D0828532

THE SENTINEL CEO

THE SENTINEL CEO

PERSPECTIVES ON SECURITY, RISK, AND LEADERSHIP IN A POST-9/11 WORLD

WILLIAM G. PARRETT

JOHN WILEY & SONS, INC.

Library of Congress Cataloging-in-Publication Data:

Parrett, William G.
    The sentinel CEO : perspectives on security, risk, and leadership in a post-9/11 world / William G. Parrett.
        p. cm.
    ISBN 978-0-470-12541-0 (c;loth)
    1. Crisis management. 2. Risk management. 3. Corporations–Security measures–Management. 4. Industries–Security measures–Management. I. Title.
    HD49.P368 2007
    658.4'7–dc22

                                                    2007017804

For my mentor and friend Ray Spinola and for my partner and colleague Mark Layton, in thanks for all their guidance and support

CONTENTS

PREFACE: THE LESSONS OF 1993

The day had started in typical fashion: I was late. While my occasional tardiness, admittedly, can be exasperating to my colleagues, I prefer to see myself as a just-in-time executive. Remembering at the last minute that my automobile lease was up that day, I dropped the car off at the dealer and took a taxi to the World Trade Center, in downtown Manhattan. Little did I know that if I'd driven to work, I wouldn't have had a car to drive home. But I'm getting ahead of the story.

As legions of people remember, the twin towers of the World Trade Center were equipped with an array of elevators that can most generously be described as inspiring—and, from the underground garage, it took three banks of them to get to my office on the 100th floor of World Trade 2, nearly a quarter-mile up. For first-time visitors, these rides were not easily forgotten. It wasn't so much the speed with which the large elevators moved, although they rocketed skyward at 27 feet per second, but rather their disconcerting sway and the banging sounds they made along the way made them memorable.

I'd arrived in the office just after 12 noon to join a meeting in progress when we felt the building jerk and then heard strange, unidentifiable noises. A certain amount of movement in the twin towers was not unusual; in high winds, the buildings could oscillate as much as three feet. Even so, no one who worked there confused flexibility with fragility: We knew that the towers had been built to withstand hurricane-force gales and even the impact of a Boeing 707. Swaying was normal, we'd been told, and nothing to worry about.

Still, several of us left the conference room to see what was happening. In the corridors we saw people milling about, but no one had the faintest clue as to what had happened. I returned to my meeting and excused myself so I could investigate. Within a minute, I spotted our emergency response team gathering down the hall. Walking down the hall to join them, I could see that the lights were now out and that smoke was beginning to create a haze on the floor.

Our team of experts had already made the decision to evacuate the building. I took the order to get out seriously and returned to the conference room to pass along the instruction. My partners and I then systematically checked each floor to make sure everyone complied with the evacuation order.

We fanned out through the eight floors occupied by the Deloitte U.S. firm—93, 94, 95, and 97 through 101. At that time of day, more than half of our 2,400 people were working on those floors. In the office setup we had then—when office space was less expensive—we had a fair amount of open space compared with today, so we had to be systematic as we made our way through the office areas.

Once the evacuation order was given, our people began to move down the stairs. There wasn't much room to maneuver. Each step could accommodate no more than two people at a time, and there were some workers with disabilities and special needs. Since more than 20,000 people normally worked in World Trade 2 every day, permanent emergency stations had been established on the 78th and 44th floors, where fire, police, and medical personnel were available.

As we slowly worked our way down, no one knew what was happening, although we were confident that we would find out when we reached 78. But when we finally made it to 78, there were no emergency responders in sight. The station was empty. At this point, I really began to worry. At 78 we had to leave the stairwell, enter the floor, and then resume our descent down another staircase. We would have to repeat this maneuver on 44 as well. It took us well over three hours to make our way down to the mezzanine.

Once outside on West Street, I saw a scene that I will never forget: police cars, fire trucks, ambulances, and rescue vehicles of all kinds, chaotically parked in a tableau that looked like something out of a misdirected Hollywood disaster movie. They were from every borough and from throughout the tri-state area, and each vehicle had its own borough or town seal. The vehicles formed a panoply of colors that stood out against the gray concrete forest of lower Manhattan. Glass was falling to the sidewalk—much of it the result of people smashing windows with chairs.

Within the next few hours I would learn that there had been a terrorist attack on the World Trade Center. And though I didn't realize it at the time, the lives of us all would never be the same again. Of one thing I was sure: we would never return to the World Trade Center.

It was February 26, 1993.

****

Although those who had experienced firsthand the events of 1993 were better equipped to deal with September 11, 2001, no one was truly prepared for it. The tragedy of 9/11 proved to be an event beyond all imagining—one that changed our universe in 16 minutes.

In the wake of that terrible day, Americans have had to question some of their most basic assumptions. For one thing, we've come to understand that attacks like these are not confined to foreign countries; they can and will happen within our own borders. And we have shifted our focus from the past to the future—from parsing the details of past acts of terrorism to determining where the next ones will occur.

In the years following the bombing of 1993, the Deloitte U.S. firm outgrew its space in the World Trade Center and relocated across West Street to the newly opened World Financial Center. Thus, while our offices suffered heavy damage on 9/11, we were spared the devastating losses that befell so many of our downtown neighbors. Even so, structurally joined at the hip as we were to the twin towers, our business and our psyches were directly and irreversibly affected by the day's events.

Like countless other companies in Manhattan and throughout the United States, Deloitte U.S. has since invested heavily—more heavily than one could ever have foreseen—in security upgrades. And, like many CEOs, I have mulled over the meaning of the verb *invest*, with its suggestion of targeted returns and bottom-line results. Is there a return on investment, or ROI, for security and risk management?

There are those who regard such spending as largely unproductive. They are concerned about enormous outlays of money that, in a sense, give back nothing constructive, do not improve our quality of life, and do not add to shareholder value in any way. Others believe just as strongly that an investment in heightened security and better risk management can yield a rich array of benefits that ultimately go to the bottom line.

As CEO of Deloitte Touche Tohmatsu, I can't say with any absolute conviction that more money and time have been invested in security enhancements than will ever be recovered. But neither can I be certain that enough has been invested. What I do know is this: not making that investment is not an option.

I know too that Deloitte's determination to maintain "business as usual" must be tempered with adjustments and accommodations to work routines. At some companies, business travelers have gravitated increasingly to "safe" countries, avoiding countries perceived as trouble spots. Deloitte too has made the decision not to assign people to certain jurisdictions because doing so would, quite frankly, put them in harm's way. Yet, this is an unfortunate if inevitable trend, because, to the extent that Western businesspeople shy away from certain underdeveloped parts of the world, those countries will be deprived of the economic stimulation they need to prosper.

Meanwhile, we confront the reality of a changed world even in the mundane details of our daily lives. One of the heaviest, if least quantifiable, costs we've incurred is the erosion of our sense of freedom and innocence, brought about by the creation, however necessary, of elaborate security systems and protocols. We see a barrier—concrete, electronic, or metaphoric—and it puts us on guard against others. Suddenly, the stranger in our midst has become the enemy.

In a real sense, we began waking up to a disquieting new reality long before 9/11. At the JP Morgan offices at 23 Wall Street, a short walk from Ground Zero, you can still see scarring and pockmarks left in the exterior walls by a bomb detonated there on September 16, 1920—81 years, nearly to the day, before 9/11. That earlier attack injured hundreds and took 33 lives. Just two years after the bombing of the World Trade Center in 1993, American terrorists wrote yet another chapter in mayhem when they blew up the Alfred P. Murrah Federal Building in Oklahoma City.

According to local news dispatches, the smoke had barely cleared and the search for victims had just ended when a caller tipped off the police in Austin, Texas, to the presence of a car bomb at a local music festival. In Omaha at around the same time, an enraged homeowner warned city officials of his plans to blow up the

Douglas County Courthouse unless his property taxes were lowered. A parochial school in Tucson was subjected to a bomb scare; so was the Criminal Justice Center in Memphis. In scores of other cities across the country, similar copycat threats were phoned in, checked out, and, ultimately, dismissed. But the message was clear: America's heartland, like its cities, was no longer safe from terrorism.

****

1920, 1993, 1995 . . . 2001, 2003, 2004, 2005, 2006 . . . Terrorism has been a part of the American and global landscape for longer than we commonly recognize. Yet I think it's fair to say that the changes we're now seeing in America's business climate are very much a 21st-century phenomenon. In the globalized environment in which many businesses now operate, risks of all kinds—from physical to fiscal—continue to top the corporate agenda. Information now travels far and fast. Secrecy, which was once a given of risk management, is ever more difficult to maintain. It follows, then, that much of the received wisdom about security and risk management needs to be revisited, and that new approaches are in order. Therein is the rationale for this book. I thought it would be worthwhile and instructive to explore some of these changes from the informed perspective of CEOs and others guiding corporations and shaping their strategy.

With that purpose in mind, my colleagues interviewed CEOs, chief security officers, academics, and others over the course of two years. Were they running their companies differently? I wanted to know. What kinds of new strategic decisions were they making? Who were they relying on to identify threats, assess security, and protect their companies' human and physical assets? What was their take on the new challenges the global war on terror is creating for today's business leaders? Did they believe U.S. businesses could continue to prosper abroad against the backdrop of highly confrontational foreign policy? And finally, is this new paradigm of U.S. business leadership sustainable, thanks to immigration and education, or will China and India take the lead?

This book examines some of these contemporary issues that affect the conduct of both global and American business and with which Deloitte member firms deal on a daily basis. Recently, Deloitte Touche Tohmatsu published, in conjunction with the Economist Intelligence Unit, two studies in 2004 and 2007 on the understanding that boards of directors had of the indicators of corporate success. Titled *In the Dark*, the studies showed a disconcerting gap between responsibility and understanding.

The Sentinel CEO is by no means intended to be exhaustive or encyclopedic in its scope. Rather, it focuses on two broad issues of compelling interest and significance: (1) the evolution of corporate security and risk management into an executive-level strategic function; and (2) dealing with the unexpected.

The book begins, in Chapter One, with discussions and personal insights from a variety of CEOs about their security and risk responsibilities in the context of an integrated security strategy. Drawing on these discussions,

Chapter Two sets out a broad framework for understanding security and risk issues. Chapter Three considers the special role of the chief security officer and the specific issue of the return on investment of a fully developed security and risk strategy. These three chapters make up Part 1.

Part 2 of the book—consisting of Chapters Four, Five, Six, and Seven—focuses on several examples of the new threats to business posed by globalization and how to address them. Chapter Four addresses some of the broad challenges of China and India from a comparative and historical perspective. Chapter Five considers the challenges to American—and more generally Western—brands in a volatile political world where the forces and boundaries of antiglobalization, anti-Americanism, and an array of ideologies including radical Islam sometimes converge to pose significant challenges to the conduct of business. Chapter Six pursues the discipline required to "imagine the unimaginable" by looking more closely at the dangers—real and imagined—of avian influenza. Chapter Seven delves into the precarious balance between security and maintaining America's ability to attract and retain foreign talent.

Part 3, "The Way Forward," begins with Chapter Eight, which establishes some of the fundamentals of sustainability. Chapter Nine, serving as a conclusion, offers some suggestions for what constitutes sustainable leadership in an age when business is confronted with new risks and challenges but also with unprecedented opportunity.

I earn my living by advising companies and providing recommendations that will, ideally, improve their business performance. In this capacity, I find that listening often takes precedence over speaking—and asking the right questions is often more productive than trying to provide the right answers. Those principles have been applied in gathering the insights of the individuals quoted in these pages. In many ways, *The Sentinel CEO* is as much their book as mine, which is exactly how it should be.

In addition, I would like to gratefully acknowledge the guidance of Mark Layton, Global Leader for the Enterprise Risk Services (ERS) practice, and his team, as well as the assistance of Dave Crutcher, Mark Felton, and Michel Le Gall in the preparation of this book.

WILLIAM G. PARRETT
Chief Executive Officer,
Deloitte Touche Tohmatsu,
New York City

December 2006

ABOUT THE AUTHOR

William G. Parrett is Chief Executive Officer of Deloitte (Deloitte Touche Tohmatsu), the global professional services organization, and Senior Partner of Deloitte & Touche USA LLP. In a career that spans more than three decades and markets around the world, Mr. Parrett has advised many of the largest and most respected companies. Active in both business and philanthropic arenas, he is a frequent speaker at prominent business forums and serves, among other roles, as Chairman of the United States Council for International Business and as a member of the Board of Trustees of Carnegie Hall.

ABOUT DELOITTE

Deloitte refers to one or more of Deloitte Touche Tohmatsu (DTT), a Swiss Verein, its member firms, and their respective subsidiaries and affiliates. DTT is an organization of member firms around the world devoted to excellence in providing professional services and advice, focused on client service through a global strategy executed locally in nearly 140 countries. With access to the deep intellectual capital of approximately 135,000 people worldwide, Deloitte delivers services in four professional areas—audit, tax, consulting, and financial advisory services—and serves more than 80 percent of the world's largest companies, as well as large national enterprises, public institutions, locally important clients, and successful, fast-growing global growth companies. Services are not provided by the DTT Verein, and, for regulatory and other reasons, certain member firms do not provide services in all four professional areas.

As a Swiss Verein (association), neither DTT nor any of its member firms has any liability for each other's acts or omissions. Each of the member firms is a separate and independent legal entity operating under the names "Deloitte," "Deloitte & Touche," "Deloitte Touche Tohmatsu," or other related names.

For the convenience of the reader, a member firm of DTT in a particular country is identified in the body of this publication by the word "Deloitte" coupled with a country name (e.g., Deloitte Greece), in lieu of using the actual legal name of the member firm of DTT in that country. In many countries, services may be provided by the actual member firms but could also be provided in addition by—or solely by—subsidiaries or affiliates of the Deloitte member firm in that country, which are often organized as separate legal entities. Each of these separate legal entities is liable for its own acts or omissions and not those of other separate legal entities. Additionally, for purposes of this publication only, individuals are identified by their name and the nomenclature discussed earlier for referring to a Deloitte member firm, whether that individual is a partner, principal, shareholder, member, director, or employee of that Deloitte member firm or one or more of its subsidiaries or affiliates (e.g., Zoe

Poulos, Deloitte Greece). For example, and specifically with respect to the United States, Deloitte & Touche USA LLP is the member firm of Deloitte Touche Tohmatsu. Services in the United States are provided by Deloitte & Touche LLP, Deloitte Tax LLP, Deloitte Consulting LLP, and Deloitte Financial Advisory Services LLP. All of these U.S. entities are referred to in this publication as "Deloitte United States."

DISCLAIMER

The information contained herein is furnished by DTT and is intended to provide general information on a particular subject or subjects and is not an exhaustive treatment of such subject(s).

Accordingly, the information is not intended to constitute accounting, tax, legal, investment, consulting, or other professional advice or services. The information is not intended to be relied upon as the sole basis for any decision that may affect you or your business. Before making any decision or taking any action that might affect your personal finances or business, you should consult a qualified professional adviser.

The information contained herein is provided as is, and DTT makes no express or implied representations or warranties regarding this information. Without limiting the foregoing, DTT does not warrant that the information contained herein will be error-free or will meet any particular criteria of performance or quality. DTT expressly disclaims all implied warranties, including, without limitation, warranties of merchantability, title, fitness for a particular purpose, noninfringement, compatibility, security, and accuracy.

Your use of the information contained herein is at your own risk, and you assume full responsibility and risk of loss resulting from the use thereof. DTT will not be liable for any special, indirect, incidental, consequential, or punitive damages or any other damages whatsoever, whether in an action of contract, statute, tort (including, without limitation, negligence), or otherwise, relating to the use of the information contained herein.

The views, policies, and practices expressed in this book are the author's own and should not be interpreted as necessarily representing the views, policies, or practices, express or implied, of DTT and its member firms or any of their respective subsidiaries or affiliates. The views, policies, and practices expressed by an individual or organization participating herein are solely those of said individual or organization and not of the author, DTT and its member firms, or any of their respective subsidiaries or affiliates.

If any of the foregoing is not fully enforceable for any reason, the remainder shall nonetheless continue to apply.

PART ONE

UNDERSTANDING SECURITY AND RISK MANAGEMENT

Ask any business leader to define *security* or *risk management*, and you are very likely to receive a different response or nuance every time. That's because despite the wide use of expressions like security, risk management, and enterprise risk management (ERM) there is no standard or accepted definition.

As a business imperative, security and risk management and even ERM have been discussed for more than a decade. In some business sectors, notably financial services and energy, most industry-specific risks are managed using sophisticated models that rely on an advanced understanding of probability and statistics. Other companies, such as those in the service or consumer business sectors, may have less experience and a less elaborate approach to security and risk management. For them, there is a pressing need to develop a fuller and more robust appreciation of risk management.

That being said, it is probably also true to say that few companies manage the full spectrum of risk or adequately

1

assess and address risk intelligently from all perspectives and quarters. Even financial services companies may have a full grasp of interest rates, currency, and credit risk, but how many of them have suffered significant losses from catastrophic events—such as natural disasters, terrorist attacks, and other threats to business continuity—by failing to develop contingency plans for such occurrences? There is another example: Many companies anticipated the transition to e-commerce, but how many suffered a loss of reputation and customers because they failed to protect online customer data adequately?

Every company that charts its progress in risk management will find itself in a different location vis-à-vis competitors, depending on the business challenges it faces and the competencies and capabilities it possesses. But every organization that eventually learns to manage risk intelligently will need to address a variety of issues. Organizations that are most effective and efficient at managing risks in terms of both existing assets and future growth will, in the long run, outperform those that are less so. Simply put, companies make money by taking risks and lose money by failing to manage risks.

How does one define *risk*? Risk is the potential for loss caused by an event (or series of events) that can adversely affect the achievement of a company's objectives. This broad definition accommodates both the protection of existing assets and the enhancement of future growth objectives. Therefore, effective security and risk management involves not just the desire to avoid something negative (say, to prevent a hacker from accessing your customer information) but also the need to attain something positive (say, to successfully integrate an acquired company). Smart risk managers view risk not just as vulnerability to the downside but also as preparedness for the upside. That distinction is vital. Effective security and risk management embrace both an ability to anticipate and react to market opportunities and a readiness for potentially devastating business disruptions.

The chapters in this section will provide insights on an array of risk issues and will suggest some possible ways of creating a risk-intelligent organization.

1

CEO REFLECTIONS FROM THE FRONT: INTEGRATED SECURITY AND RISK MANAGEMENT

The truth is in the details. With that in mind, this chapter shares the personal insights and reflections of a small but diverse group of business leaders, from various backgrounds, on how the CEO, and the company he or she manages, can come to terms with a broad range of risks. The personal stories and perspectives of the executives interviewed for this book were at once varied and also very consistent. Virtually all of the CEOs agreed that, as a corporate community, we need to understand the challenge of terrorism more clearly, define it in the right terms, and go after the root causes that give rise to terrorists. From a business perspective, we need to gain technical competence to deal with threats from those who would seek to harm us. We need to understand and embrace local cultural values in order to operate successfully abroad. And governments need to collaborate with our partners, not strong-arm them.

DO THE RIGHT THING
Robert Benmosche
Former Chairman and CEO, MetLife[1]

Robert Benmosche grew up fast. "I suppose I had to," he said. "I was ten when my father died; my mother supported the family from that point on. I had to pick up street sense in a hurry." In time, Benmosche's street sense evolved into street smarts (as in Wall Street), and into the leadership qualities needed to run one of the country's largest insurance companies. The death of his father taught young Benmosche an early lesson in how a single unpredictable calamity can change everything in an instant.

This type of situation is why there are insurance companies. It's hardly a surprise that the insurance business is on the front lines of the war on terrorism. Insured losses from the attacks of September 11 were a staggering US$32.5 billion.[2] But, then, the industry is accustomed to big-ticket losses: the hurricanes of 2004 and 2005 caused untold billions of dollars of damage in Florida, Louisiana, and Mississippi; the specific price tag for hurricanes Katrina, Rita, and Wilma in 2005 has reached well more than US$100 billion.[3]

"Wall Street has been after me for four years now to sell it," Benmosche said of the MetLife subsidiary that helped cover homeowner and business losses after four hurricanes struck Florida in 2004, causing more than US$8 billion in losses. "But we've turned it around from a business that did US$40 million to US$50 million in after-tax profit to this year (2005), where we'll do up to US$100 million."

Remarkably, the subsidiary has accomplished this despite its insistence on not requiring multiple deductibles on homes damaged by multiple hurricanes. "One of our core values is personal responsibility—the idea that people count," said Benmosche. "You've still got to manage volatility and make sure you turn a profit. But our Florida team decided—independent of any management directives—that it simply isn't right to collect multiple deductibles when the same home is battered by multiple hurricanes. I think doing the right thing is its own reward. Of course, it also benefits us as a company—reputationally and financially."

This is a "culture point" at MetLife that originated long before Benmosche arrived there from PaineWebber in 1995. When the 703 survivors of the *Titanic* steamed into New York harbor aboard the cruise ship *Carpathia* in 1912, the Metropolitan Life Insurance Company at 1 Madison Avenue opened its doors. Then the tallest structure in the world, "the building was about the only place at the time where all the survivors could be properly looked after." In the immediate aftermath of the September 11 attacks, the company again opened its doors to survivors. "It's not something that we all sat down and had to figure out," recalled Benmosche, who was in Europe at the time of the attack. "Everybody had to act quickly and instinctively." It's one thing to provide shelter and aid to the survivors of terrorist attacks and something else to combat terrorism at its roots. Does the business community have a responsibility in helping with the latter effort?

Like many other American business leaders, Benmosche is deeply troubled by his belief that the United States neither understands the enemy nor has devised policies that address the underlying causes of global terrorism. The evidence is everywhere—in the Balkans, in Chechnya, in the Middle East, and even in Cuba, just 90 miles from U.S. shores. "It's absurd for us to labor under the delusion that deprivation and repression will eventually induce the Cubans to overthrow their government," Benmosche said. Rather, the United States should do everything in its power to encourage the growth of Cuba's middle class and foster a society where citizens can aspire to a higher quality of life. "We have to give societies a chance to have something to fight for—a reason to fight to protect what they cherish," he said.

"WE'RE ONLY AS STRONG AS THE WEAKEST OF US"
Michael Morris
Chairman, President, and CEO, American Electric Power Company[4]

Michael Morris joined American Electric Power (AEP) just a few years ago from Northeast Utilities System, a much smaller business in Connecticut. Now, he runs a company that forms the backbone of America's power grid from Ohio to the East Coast. Most of AEP's more than 60 power plants are coal-fired; only one is nuclear-fueled. While Morris is a champion of clean nuclear energy, he acknowledges that "our industry in general and this company in particular are obviously concerned about the security of our nuclear facilities. How safe are they?"

One of the standards by which the safety of a nuclear plant is measured is its ability to withstand a direct hit from a commercial airplane, such as a Boeing 707 or 727. But whether it can survive the impact of a 767, 777, 787, an Airbus A380, or any of the other supersized aircraft that didn't exist when many nuclear plants were designed is questionable. In any event, Morris's biggest concern has to do with a military-style attack, which might—or might not—involve commercial jets.

"Most nuclear plants are located on large bodies of water and thus are accessible from both land and water as well as from the air," Morris explained as he sat in AEP's expansive offices in Columbus, Ohio. "So, in the wake of 9/11, we took a hard look and concluded that better training and more armed guards were essential." At AEP's nuclear facility, he said, the difference between current security levels and what they were like pre-9/11 "is like night and day."

As devastating as a direct hit on a nuclear plant would be, Morris, like many in industry and government, is most worried about the disruption of the energy transmission and distribution system. An attack on a nuclear facility, unless the core was exposed—which is highly unlikely, even after a direct hit by a plane—wouldn't disrupt the distribution of power; the various grids would automatically adjust and carry on as normal. "If some-one wanted to really dent the U.S. economy, a handful of pointed attacks on critical substations could leave you with a seriously affected economy," Morris said. "It's conceivable that energy wouldn't be available in pockets of the country for months, if not years."

He's not just spinning tales: On August 14, 2003, in less than a minute, 50 million people in the United States lost power. It was a relief to learn that the blackout was the result of human error and not sabotage—and, luckily, the nation rebounded and got back on line quickly. But in places like Cleveland, where the municipal water supply is dependent on electrical power from the grid, a sus-tained lapse in power could have serious consequences for public health. "We're only as strong as the weakest of us," said Morris.

The structure of the U.S. utility industry puts tremen-dous pressure on management to be conversant in highly technical matters and to make decisions for the very long term. How do power companies accomplish this? How do they set policy and deal with the management and safety issues of nuclear and other facilities?

Although the newest nuclear facility was ordered for construction more than three decades ago, there are 66 existing plants throughout the United States. AEP, which operates one, has established a special nuclear oversight committee, whose members include scientists, CEOs, and others—such as Kathryn D. Sullivan, CEO of the Center of Science & Industry; and Richard Sandor, Chairman and CEO of Chicago Climate Exchange, Inc.

AEP also has a public policy committee that reviews the overall safety of the system. From Morris's perspective, one committee is good, but two committees are better: "Years ago, it was hard for any one person, sitting on a utility board, to form a comprehensive view of an energy system," he said. "You'd look at a map or a photograph and get an idea, but you'd never see the big picture. With two committees—one for oversight, one looking at safety—you get a much richer and integrated view of the system. And that translates into a much higher level of security." It is clearly essential that utilities invest to secure nuclear plants against external threats and internal sabotage, but what matters most, said Morris, "in the final analysis is the workforce culture of safety."

Like many of the executives interviewed, Morris felt that the biggest threat to United States security is the paucity of our knowledge about our enemies. "I don't think we understand what drives terrorists," he said. "We're not clear on the emotions involved on the other side of the equation. There's almost a whole generation of people who have no hope, no future, no vision. They have none of the things that motivate you and me to strive for improvement, and those things are of real concern to me."

"WE HAVE A CULTURE THAT IS INSULAR"
James F. Orr
Chairman and CEO, Convergys[5]

Of all the companies discussed in this chapter, Jim Orr's is probably the most far-flung geographically.

Name a country, and, chances are, Convergys has people there—in India, the Philippines, Israel, Malaysia, and dozens of hot spots. But not all of the company's employees are Americans: Convergys is the epitome of outsourcing.

Convergys is a global leader in providing customer care, human resources, and billing services. Convergys combines specialized knowledge and expertise with solid execution to deliver outsourced solutions, consulting services, and software support. Convergys serves the world's leading companies in many industries including communications, financial services, and consumer products. Among their clients are companies like American Express, AT&T, Sprint Nextel, Time Warner, ComCast, DuPont, Whirlpool, and DirecTV.

Unlike other global companies based in the United States, Convergys tends to fly under the radar—principally because of the nature of its work, which is typically invisible to the general public—and it has had to make substantial investments in recruiting and training employees abroad. It also invests heavily in maintaining safe environments for thousands of workers in myriad worksites, many of which appear on other companies' "do not travel" lists.

"We have a lot of locations outside the United States, so we need to be sensitive to global events and particularly to cultural differences and social norms," said Orr at Convergys's headquarters in Cincinnati, Ohio. "Security considerations aside, we have to maintain an increased awareness of the impact of U.S. foreign policy or anything that affects the places where we operate. Admittedly, not everyone will understand the way things are decided and done in the United States, just as we might not fully grasp the underlying rationale for decisions in Afghanistan or Uzbekistan. But U.S. companies doing business abroad have a special obligation to be attuned to local mores and standards," he said—at least if they expect to be effective globally. What it comes down to is "a need for a much broader worldview than most Americans have."

Because Convergys provides outsourced business solutions, its workforce comprises a vast array of faiths, nationalities, ethnic backgrounds, and political sensibilities. Inevitably, that degree of diversity has a powerful impact on the way the company does business. "If you're going to be in India and employ Indians, or be in the Philippines and employ Filipinos, you need to understand that the people you're employing aren't American—and that they're going to have a somewhat different perspective on a lot of things," Orr said.

Sadly, a lack of understanding has helped create the soil in which terrorism has taken root. As noted earlier, terrorism is hardly a contemporary phenomenon, but it is widespread today, and far more multiform than ever before. Most often it involves the killing of innocents, although economic or cultural terrorism rarely results in loss of life: "France has been very concerned about the loss of its culture to things like McDonald's and Pizza Hut, and even the corruption of the French language," said Orr. "Do people react to that? Yes. And is that reaction negative? Oftentimes it is. But it doesn't lead to terror." That depends on your definition. To Orr, some of the logic that is fueling the radical elements of Islam is like other forms of fundamentalism that often have a lack of tolerance for those with a different view. What sets it apart from other terrorist movements—such as the Basques in Spain, the Irish Republican Army (IRA) in Northern Ireland, or even the narco-terrorists in Latin America—is its borderless scope.

Despite the clashes of culture and commercialism that have always pitted the United States against nationalist sentiments, Orr sees 9/11 as a watershed. "The world will never be the same," he said. "Our lives will never be the same. Events like 9/11 simply shine a very bright light on the changes happening all over the world." The sad irony, he felt, is that Americans have so much to learn: "We have a culture that is insular, and even though we have so much more access to communication and information, much of the American culture still lacks any kind of global perspective."

Clearly, some companies have trimmed their sails in response to the ongoing "war on terror," shutting down operations in risky places, and expanding their list of "do not travel" zones. "For businesspeople, I generally don't see the war on terror as either personalized or translated into some reluctance to do business," he said. "Companies are doing what they have to."

At Convergys, a new focus on security has been built into day-to-day practices: more (and more visible) security personnel, more frequent communication with employees, and more security briefings for people traveling abroad. Orr said that he's personally spending more time on security issues and that the company's investment in security upgrades has increased sharply in recent years. "I think there's a strong likelihood that there will be another attack, in some form, on the United States," he said. "We don't know where or when, and we're doing everything we can to prevent it and to minimize the damage. But I suspect that one way or another there will be some event in the United States."

But Orr is not given to despair. "One of the things I hope will come about is that the U.S. electorate becomes much more aware of the importance of understanding international events—and of international policy as a qualification for candidates. Many times we've elected presidents who have relatively little knowledge of foreign affairs. I think the time is past when we can afford that."

Orr is a thoughtful leader and citizen whose tone sounds troubled when he's talking about the barriers that divide us. "When someone reached out an arm to help you in one of the stairwells of the World Trade Center, you didn't look to see the color of the hand," he said. "The emergency workers, many of whom gave their lives, didn't care whether you were black or white, Jew, Muslim, or Christian. In my mind, politically, I think one of our biggest issues is that there's so much effort focused on dividing people. I really would just love to see a day when our politicians were focused on what they were going to do for the United States in an inclusive, not exclusive, way."

PIERCING THE PULL OF THE ORDINARY
Howard Lutnick
CEO, Cantor Fitzgerald[6]

Perhaps no name is more closely linked to the events of September 11, 2001, than Cantor Fitzgerald. Occupying five floors near the top of the World Trade Center's North Tower—above the point of impact—the financial services firm lost all but 302 of its 960 employees in the attack.

"There's no question that 9/11 is a part of us and always will be," said CEO Howard Lutnick, whose brother Gary and best friend, Doug Gardner, were among those who died on that day. "But it doesn't define us." The interview was being conducted in a third-floor conference room in the midtown Manhattan building that has been Cantor's headquarters since 2005. Lutnick appeared satisfied with the layout and decor of the new space, but there was a wistful note to his description of the breathtaking vistas from the 105th floor of the World Trade Center.

"When the weather was clear, you could see almost sixty miles," he recalled. "There were mornings when you'd get to the office early and there'd be a perfect blue sky above, a solid bank of clouds below, and the tip of the Empire State Building sticking up through the clouds, like Jack and the beanstalk." In the 18 years during which he worked in the twin towers, Lutnick never took those views for granted; they were so heartbreaking in their beauty "that they pierced the pull of the ordinary."

Following 9/11, Lutnick resolved to wage his own battle against the pull of the ordinary. He would do so by presiding over Cantor's rebirth—and by ensuring that the families of the employees who had died were looked after.

"In a very short time, we suffered a corporate physical and personal disaster beyond anyone's imagination," he said. "When have a company's entire board of directors, its president, vice chairman, chief operating officer, and CFO all died on the same day?" Of the employees who survived, "there weren't any who didn't lose somebody close to them."

In the wake of the attack, Cantor faced a choice. The firm could try to fight its way back to the top of its industry, trying to be the company it had been on September 10, 2001. But there was little enthusiasm for spending the next five years "just getting back to where we'd been," Lutnick said. "In effect, we'd been knocked off the top of the mountain. But instead of trying to climb back up, we decided to strap on skis and ski on down—to take the parts of the company that remained and build from there."

By any rational measure, the destruction of the World Trade Center "should have been the end of our enterprise," Lutnick said. Eighty-two of the eighty-six people in the corporate bond division died; the four who survived "simply weren't enough to form the nucleus of a new operation." Ultimately they left the firm, as did the secretaries and assistants of the executives who had arrived at the office before them that day and been killed.

"But the one thing we knew was that we had to survive as a company," Lutnick said. That determination came as much from a sense of personal accountability as from business considerations: "First and foremost, we needed to get back to work so that we could care for the families of those we lost." Toward that end, Cantor made an extraordinary commitment: to set aside 25% of its profits for those families for the next five years. Importantly, the payments would begin at once—"when the families needed the money most"—rather than be deferred until the firm could regain its footing financially.

To those who worked at Cantor, the commitment was less extraordinary than predictable. This was a firm that had prided itself on a policy of "encouraged nepotism"—the active recruitment of employees' friends and relatives at every level of the organization. The result was "an unusually strong personal and professional connection among employees," Lutnick said.

Well into 2002, the *New York Times* published daily profiles of people killed in the attack. "In at least half of the Cantor profiles, you'd see the words, 'He—or she—loved the job'," Lutnick said. "That tells you a lot about our work environment. People felt an exceptional connection to each other, and that made our desire to help the families so much stronger. It wasn't just your coworker's family you were helping. The guy in the next office who was killed could have been your best friend, or an old high school buddy."

Meanwhile, the firm set about reconstituting itself. All notions of trying to salvage the U.S. interdealer business were quickly scrapped; instead, all of the U.S. operations would be built on the foundation of Cantor's institutional equities sales and trading business. At the same time, the firm would maintain its interdealer business in Europe and continue to migrate interdealer fixed-income business to its electronic trading subsidiary, eSpeed. Over the next two and a half years, Cantor expanded and strengthened its institutional sales and trading franchise worldwide, building on the remnants of existing businesses where possible and also moving into new areas, such as institutional fixed-income sales and trading, market commentary, and asset management.

"Essentially, we took the business down to its foundation and then built it up again—first making sure that the foundation was rock-solid," Lutnick said. By the beginning of 2004, we felt we were on solid-enough ground to start adding management and moving forward." By the summer of that year, "we were ready to slam on the gas. It was a time of new directions, aggressive expansion, and absolute confidence." Since then, Cantor has grown rapidly, adding 1,500 new employees (1,000 in New York alone); it now employs some 2,900 people globally. It is a bigger company than it was in September 2001—in some ways the same, but in many others, remarkably changed.

Like the Deloitte U.S. firm, Cantor had suffered serious damage to its offices in the bombing of the World Trade Center in 1993. "We learned a number of lessons from that attack—the first of which is that most disaster recovery plans are a disaster," Lutnick said. "They start from a set of theoretical notions that aren't operationally acceptable." The plan in place at the time of the attack in 1993 allowed for immediate mobilization of 70% of the firm's workforce. "But I realized that this simply wouldn't work," Lutnick said. "Unless you're prepared to deliver 100%, you're going to lose. So we put off reopening until we could operate at full capacity, six days later."

Cantor's senior management also learned to dispense with conventional notions of backup systems and shift to "concurrent computing"—the use of multiple systems operating simultaneously. When the firm lost its central technology hub on the 104th floor of the North Tower on 9/11, two others—one in New Jersey, the other in London—kept running. As a result, the firm maintained unbroken continuity in the face of unspeakable disaster. Although the firm's investment in such gold-plated redundancy clearly paid off, "this was a lesson you couldn't have drilled into my head before 1993," Lutnick said. "It would have seemed far too expensive and complex."

"The terrorists didn't set out to kill my brother and my friends or attack Cantor Fitzgerald on 9/11, even if that is what they wound up doing," he said. "They attacked us because we were American, because we lived in the West. But now they're dead. So I don't know what else I can do. Like everyone else, I screamed and cried and yelled, and punched the wall, and cried again." The attacks of 1993 and 2001 were fueled by "a hatred that has been stoked for generations and bred into children virtually from infancy," he said. "Somewhere in the Middle East, a child will be born tomorrow. Will he grow up to become a suicide bomber? Or will he think, 'Life is precious and beautiful'?"

There are no easy answers. Perhaps, as Lutnick suggested, it's already too late to get to the current generation of children. Very possibly, it will fall to their children—and to our children's children—to create a different world from the one we have. "We need to address that hatred—but the best way to address it is clearly open for debate," Lutnick said. "In the end, it may be that beating hatred philosophically is impossible. But if we beat it only with arms and strength, then we've not beaten it at all."

"TERRORISM IS A TACTIC"
John Hamre
Director, Center for Strategic and International Studies[7]

John Hamre, a former deputy secretary of defense, transformed the Center for Strategic and International Studies (CSIS), a one-time subcontractor for the U.S. Department of Defense, into one of the most respected Washington think tanks. Tackling problems as diverse as security, global warming, and water rights, the CSIS is guided by boards that read like a who's who of people in government service. Hamre considers the CSIS the federal government's strategic planning arm—not that long-term strategic planning counts very highly in Beltway circles these days, he said.

"Part of the problem with this term, 'war on terrorism,' is that it's so poorly defined," he argued. "It doesn't help you develop policy solutions. Calling something a war on terror is like calling World War II the war on the blitzkrieg." Terrorism is a tactic, Hamre contended—a modality by which people try to create political reality. Thus, "to declare war on a tactic is frankly more confusing to us than it is helpful."

What's needed, then, "is genuine clarity of our objectives—and we don't have that right now," Hamre continued. "Rather, we hew to an extreme ideological distortion of a religion that has great political currency these days, and that then plays off historic grievances, and the cultural context of Arab Islam, to create a very long-term problem." It's a problem that requires a multidimensional solution, he said, but as of yet, no one has come up with one.

Hamre supports the notion of promoting representative government in the Middle East but concedes that this is a very long-term goal: "Over the next 20 years, something like 300 million new Arabs will be born," he said. "The Middle East is a region where mothers give birth to five kids and the economies give jobs to two of them. This is not a tenable situation." Will the problems get worse before they get better? "Yes, and we're addressing them not in a holistic way but in a grandiose 'bring democracy' way. It's not working."

What bearing does all of this have on the business community? "The business community is trying to design ways to succeed inside this changing environment.

But the reality is that we're living in a world of our own paranoia." The day before the interview, a small airplane intruded on the restricted airspace of the U.S. Capitol. To Hamre, the reaction proved his point: "A Piper Cub gets lost over Washington, D.C., and we start evacuating the Capitol and the White House. My God, you're in more danger outside than inside. The Piper Cub isn't going to come through those walls. Yet what do we do? We scream 'Get out! Get out!' and run like rabbits. We've got to get a grip on the real problems we're facing. We've used vocabulary that's imprecise, and we've had a political backdrop that rewards paranoia. And that context has led us to a situation where we have remarkably little clarity in our goals as a nation to deal with this problem."

What are the real problems? "I think we have two sets of problems," he said. "Terrorism is one, but I'm not sure it's the bigger of the two. We've clearly brought on ourselves a set of staggering costs associated with preventing terrorism, but I don't think that's the great problem with our economy. The problem, rather, is that we're spending 10% more than we produce every year. How can we keep that up? That is a product of our lack of discipline as a nation; we've become a society that feels it can consume extravagantly without a worry for the future."

While Hamre is a Republican, he believes that the Republicans have erred in being dismissive about the deficit. "It's dangerously large," he said. "Yet our leaders are prepared to let our exchange rate deteriorate—to basically let foreigners finance us, and right now we're importing a lot of money that will burden our economy for a very long time." We've succeeded thus far because America is still the safest place for capital, with a relatively predictable and transparent legal system and a mature capital market, he said; our capacity to repatriate our funds, even on a diminished basis, is greater here than anyplace else in the world. "But at some point, foreigners are going to stop lending us money," he added. "So, that is the real issue—a government not willing to live within its means, spending more than it's prepared to tax. If the Europeans are always worried that our economy is imbalanced, I think they're right. I think it's a product of very deep factors that are much beyond the issue of terrorism."

Because of its historic expertise in defense and security, the CSIS came to the fore following 9/11. However, Hamre is quick to suggest that our approach to homeland security was ill-conceived: "We labored under the delusion that you can secure American soil on a parochial basis—that you can put higher fences around the border and bigger stations at the border entries, and somehow you can secure the country." Hamre argues that we are a "globally interactive society—not physically, but metaphorically. We've used a perimeter security model as the implicit model for homeland security. So, in the perimeter, security is 'I'm going to have a guard at the gate, a guard at the fence line, a guard at the edge of the property line.'"

Is there a better route to homeland security? Hamre thinks so: "We need to know, for example, through deep collaboration with intelligence and law enforcement authorities in other countries, which containers to look in," he said. "But you're not going to do that if you alienate your relations with these other countries. The problem is that our foreign policy posture has been quite alienating and completely contradictory to what we really need for a successful homeland security posture. We've had this attitude, 'You're either with us or against us,' and then we've said, 'But with us means you've got to do it precisely the way we want you to do it.' And the rest of the world said, 'I'm not against you, but I'm not going to do it that way.'"

Nor can terrorism be viewed in narrowly American terms, he said: "We've got to be just as worried about terrorism in Spain as we are about terrorism in the United States, because ultimately we're all caught in the same web. We're going to need to share information with Spain, Indonesia, and the others, because we're expecting them to share it with us. We can't then take an approach that alienates the bulk of the world and causes them to pull back from working with us. We've got to start thinking our way through this problem, not just viscerally reacting to it."

"YOU WILL SEE: THE WORLD IS GOING TO BE DIFFERENT"
Aloïs Michielsen
Chairman of the Executive Committee, Solvay[8]

It goes without saying that Europeans often have a different perspective on world affairs, economics, and politics from their American cousins. Long accustomed to terrorism on their own soil, Europeans must have considered the 9/11 attack as, in a sense, inevitable. Aloïs Michielsen is the thoughtful, soft-spoken CEO of Solvay, which is based in Brussels and is one of Europe's largest companies. Educated at the University of Chicago, Michielsen has a keen sense of America and American-style business. Still, when his wife phoned him to describe what she was witnessing on CNN, he was stunned. As a businessman, he made some quick decisions, instructing subordinates to reduce inventories at his chemical plants and tighten up working capital. He then placed a call to a top Belgian politician. The reply was something of a shock. "I asked him, 'Are you informed?' He said, 'Aloïs, in a couple of months it will be forgotten.'" To which Michielsen replied: 'I'm not so sure. I know the United States, and I know the American people. You will see, they will be fundamentally affected by this. The world is going to be different.'"

In particular, he insists, the relationship between the United States and Europe has been radically transformed. Everyone is aware of the strong disagreement about America's response to 9/11, particularly the war in Iraq, but Michielsen senses that there are also changes within companies because of the new foreign policy dynamics.

"There are a number of macroeconomic consequences as well," he said. In his view, America seems focused too intently on fighting a long war with little attention to addressing the fundamental problems of the U.S. economy: high deficits, unrestrained spending, large tax cuts, and funding of social benefits. The bottom line: "America's economy is weakening. And America's adventurist foreign policy is taking a high toll on addressing the 'internal competitiveness' of the country."

Is America still considered a leader in business and business education? "Not as much as a generation ago," he said. But the cause is not necessarily America's higher education system or its burdensome visa requirements; there is simply much greater competition for students from other countries. From Stockholm to Singapore, opportunities for high-quality graduate education have multiplied.

****

It is hardly a surprise that the word *security* came up repeatedly in conversations with CEOs. "Everyone is taking security a lot more seriously these days, whether it pertains to travel, their physical facilities, or their data," Jim Orr of Convergys noted. "There's just a much higher level of consciousness that I think exists everywhere." The added layers of protection range from low-tech measures such as checking visitors' identification to advanced technological innovations that not so long ago would have been the stuff of science fiction.

But perhaps the most significant sign of the growing importance of security has been the evolution of a new senior-level position on the corporate organization chart. As we will see in Chapters Two and Three, the chief security officer is fast becoming a key decision maker in the top management of many U.S. companies and an indispensable ally of the CEO.

NOTES

1. Interview conducted on November 16, 2004.
2. Institut Veolia Environnement, Report no. 3: "Financial protection of critical infrastructure, September 11, 2001: Insurance against a new form of terrorism." *http://www.institut.veolia.org/en/cahiers/protection-insurability-terrorism/protection-vulnerabilities/insurance-terrorism.aspx*. Direct economic losses are valued at US$80 billion.
3. *http://money.cnn.com/2005/09/02/news/katrina_estimates*
4. Interview conducted on December 8, 2004.
5. Interview conducted on December 8, 2004.
6. Interview conducted on September 8, 2005.
7. Interview conducted on May 12, 2005.
8. Interview conducted on April 25, 2005.

2

A FRAMEWORK FOR MANAGING SECURITY AND RISK

After 9/11, a special independent Congressional commission was established. Its mandate was to examine the nature of the intelligence and security lapses that had preceded the attacks. One of the principal conclusions of the commission was simple: The greatest failure had been "a failure of imagination."[1]

In the globalized environment in which many businesses now operate, risk continues to top the corporate agenda. Information now travels farther and faster than ever before. Consequently, companies are open to new types of risks and threats that were virtually unknown just 10 or 15 years ago. It follows, then, that much of the received wisdom about security and risk management needs to be revisited, and that new approaches are in order.

Drawing on the discussions with CEOs and security chiefs, some of which were presented in Chapter One, my discussion here will offer some of the broad dimensions of security and risk management and point toward some best practices. In so doing, my aim is to provide a broader framework for imagining and managing the variety of risks that modern corporations face: risks that are not isolated issues but part of a continuous spectrum of issues facing executives in the C-suite.

My aim is to advance a more refined and integrated approach to security and risk management—an approach that views them as an integral part of corporate strategy and performance; an approach that emphasizes the connection between mitigating risk and ensuring the long-term sustainability of the corporation and its ability to deliver value to its stakeholders.

IT'S DANGEROUS OUT THERE

Let's think beyond terrorism and consider one of a senior executive's worst nightmares: In just a few days, the company's share price plummets. Available credit quickly dries up. Expansion plans are put on hold. The firm takes years to recover its original value, and by the time it does so, senior management has been replaced. Unfortunately, this nightmare is all too often a reality for some of the world's largest companies. What causes major losses of shareholder value? And what steps can senior management take to minimize the risks?

Although the past does not necessarily predict the future, understanding the factors that have destroyed corporate value suggests ways that firms can reduce their vulnerability to these sudden shocks. An analysis by

Deloitte Research in the United States identified the largest one-month declines in share price for the 1,000 largest international companies (based on market value) from 1994 and 2003. The results were sobering: Almost half of the companies had lost more than 20% of their market value over a one-month period at least once in that decade relative to the Morgan Stanley Capital International (MSCI) world stock index (see Exhibit 2.1).

The losses in value were often long-lasting. For roughly one-quarter of the companies, it took longer than one year, sometimes much longer, before share prices recovered to their original levels. By the end of 2003, the share prices for almost one-quarter of the companies had still not recovered to their original levels (see Exhibit 2.2).

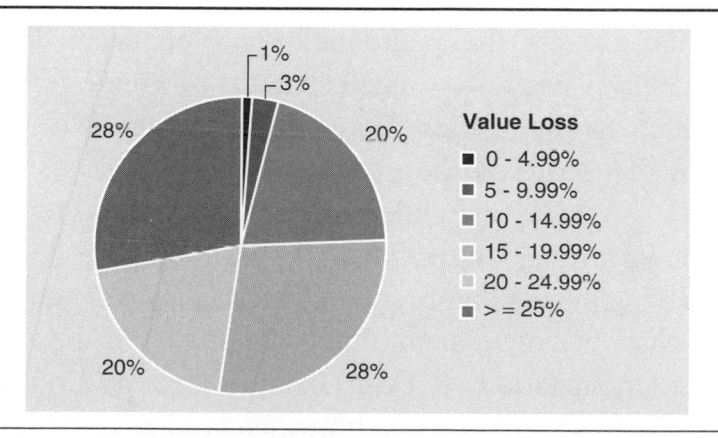

EXHIBIT 2.1 DECLINES IN SHARE PRICE AMONG LARGEST INTERNATIONAL COMPANIES, 1994–2003

Source: Deloitte Research USA, *Disarming the Value Killers: A Risk Management Study* (New York: Deloitte Development LLC, 2005), p. 2.

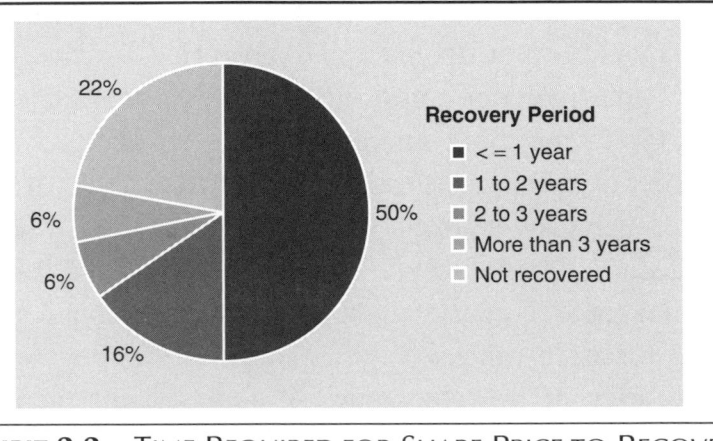

EXHIBIT 2.2   TIME REQUIRED FOR SHARE PRICE TO RECOVER,
1994–2003
Source: Deloitte Research USA, *Disarming the Value
Killers: A Risk Management Study* (New York: Deloitte
Development LLC, 2005), p. 3.

What caused these dramatic and enduring losses
in market value? To understand the origins, Deloitte
Research in the United States examined the 100 companies that suffered the greatest declines in share price
from 1994 to 2003. Public disclosures, analysts' reports,
and news articles on each firm provided insights into the
underlying events that accounted for lost value. Adapting
the framework developed by the Committee of the Spon-
soring Organizations (COSO) of the Treadway Commission, the researchers categorized events into four broad
risk categories:

1. Strategic risks, such as demand shortfalls, failures
    to address competitors' moves, or problems in exe-
    cuting mergers

2. Operational risks, such as cost overruns, accounting problems from failures in internal controls, and supply chain failures
3. Financial risks, such as high debt, inadequate reserves to manage increases in interest rates, poor financial management, and trading losses
4. External risks, such as industry crises, country-specific political or economic issues, terrorist acts, and public health crises

A detailed breakdown of the frequency of the risk events that fell into each of these categories is provided in Exhibit 2.3.

Clearly, companies are confronted by a wide variety of potential value killers. To make the challenge even

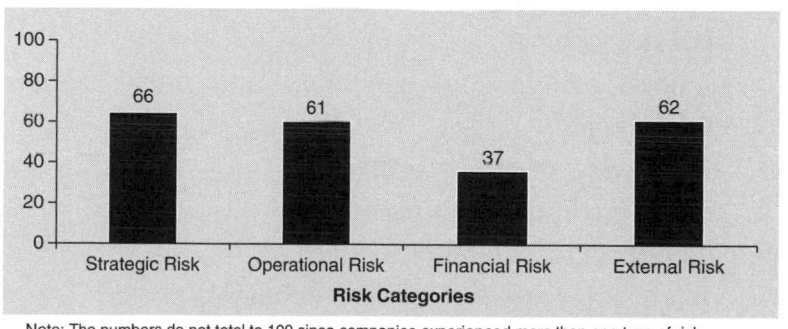

Note: The numbers do not total to 100 since companies experienced more than one type of risk.

EXHIBIT 2.3 POSSIBLE CAUSES OF VALUE LOSSES
Source: Deloitte Research USA, *Disarming the Value Killers: A Risk Management Study* (New York: Deloitte Development LLC, 2005), p. 4.

more complex, many declines in share price were the result of cascading losses from two or more types of risk events working in combination. According to the study, more than 80% of the 100 companies that suffered the greatest losses experienced risk events of more than one type. Low-probability but high-impact events also played an important role. Many companies already have some form of ERM system but still experience losses. Can these substantial value losses be prevented? Not always, but senior management and the board of directors can take steps to reduce their firm's exposure to risk and improve corporate resilience.

Taking a cue from some of the points raised by the interviewees in Chapter One, the focus of this chapter will be on the seven habits that are the foundations of good security and risk management. They can be summarized as:

1. Fostering a holistic and integrated risk management culture
2. Understanding anti-American and anti-European sentiments
3. Imagining the unimaginable
4. Business continuity planning
5. The path to risk intelligence
6. A culture rooted in ethical behavior
7. Timely information

FOSTERING A HOLISTIC AND INTEGRATED RISK MANAGEMENT CULTURE

CASE STUDY A

Following its fourth profit warning in five quarters, a major manufacturer's shares plunged by more than 25%. In total, the firm lost more than half its market value over the course of the year. Traditionally a market leader, the firm appeared to be slow to respond to the strategic risk posed by competitors aggressively introducing products with new features. But its effort to reduce costs through a radical reorganization left the firm vulnerable to operational risk as well. The firm consolidated more than 30 administrative centers into just three. Apparently, this consolidation slowed order fulfillment and billing, and increased customers' administration costs and accounts receivable.

Source: Deloitte Research USA, *Disarming the Value Killers: A Risk Management Study* (New York: Deloitte Development LLC, 2005), p. 5.

CASE STUDY B

After announcing that operating profits for the year would be 20% below expectations, a high-technology equipment manufacturer quickly lost more than 40% of its market value. One probable cause was the external risk resulting from the privatization of several telephone operators in Europe, which led to a drastic reduction in its orders. The company did not appear to incorporate its customers' vulnerability to deregulation into its own risk strategy. The impact was perhaps more pronounced because the firm faced a greater strategic risk by not having diversified its customer base from incumbent telephone operators to new competitors.

Source: Deloitte Research USA, *Disarming the Value Killers: A Risk Management Study* (New York: Deloitte Development LLC, 2005), p. 5.

Two general points need to be emphasized: (1) a new culture of security and risk management has clearly begun to emerge; and (2) this culture is cutting across the silos and discrete functions of large organizations.

In a survey conducted in 2005 by *CSO Magazine*, 59% of respondents reported that the senior management of their companies viewed the role of chief security officer (CSO) "as a strategic and permanent position."[2] It is the strategic role of the CSO that enables him or her to take on the tough challenge of breaking down the silo mind-set: the tendency to view issues of risk and security in isolation from the organization's strategy and to confine these issues to the areas of IT or physical security. The central role of the CSO goes to the heart of the matter: the central and strategic importance of security to corporate success.

To develop an appropriate, relevant, holistic approach to risk management, the following framework, which identifies four priorities and concerns, may prove useful. (Some of these points will be further elaborated later.)

The first priority is the need to identify and manage critical interdependent risks. Eighty percent of companies that suffer the greatest losses—whether security, physical, or value-based—do so because of exposure to more than one type of risk. A failure to recognize and manage the interrelationships of risk often aggravates the initial problem, and because of the unforeseen interdependence of risks, a small event may quickly grow into a company-wide, industry-wide threat.

Second, top leadership needs to create a culture that emphasizes the central importance of ethical behavior, compliance, quality control, and broader risk management. Employees' conduct, regulatory precision, and industry-appropriate risk management will help foster the right kind of risk culture. Creating a risk culture is not, however, tantamount to creating a culture marked by fear and paranoia. Instead, the ideal risk culture is characterized by a commitment to executing according to approved processes while also maintaining a balance that fosters initiative and innovation.

An additional critical element in developing an effective risk management culture and fostering appropriate leadership is setting uniform standards. Standards—whether they relate to accounting and internal control, security, or human resources—are essential for setting clear goals against which risk management practices and performance can be measured and adjusted. If agreed-upon standards are lacking, the chance of misunderstandings and risk failure increases considerably, both within a company and across many industries and professions.

Third, there is a need to proactively address low-frequency, but high-impact, risks. Some of the greatest losses in value or capital occur because of exceptional events: systems failures, financial crises, or terrorist attacks. This point needs special attention and is addressed at greater length in a following section.

Fourth, companies need to improve their internal information and communications systems to ensure that senior management and the board of directors receive accurate, nearly real-time information on the causes of, financial impact of, and possible solutions to problems of risk and control. This point goes directly to the ability of the company to capture and manage a broad variety of nonfinancial data crucial to long-term sustainability. This topic is discussed in later chapters.

These four categories can provide a broad structure within which the appropriate integrated risk management culture can be shaped. It goes without saying, though, that each industry or locale has specific risks that need to be addressed and for which contingencies and answers need to be developed. An integrated approach to risk must also be attentive to the cultural dimension of business—an intangible, perhaps, but nonetheless an important dimension of doing business globally.

UNDERSTANDING ANTI-AMERICAN AND ANTI-EUROPEAN SENTIMENTS

Western corporations, and more specifically American corporations and executives, need to reevaluate the nature of their roles abroad. American and European business executives can no longer simply consider themselves representatives of a certain company. Whether they like it or not, they are in many ways ambassadors of their countries. In this sense, when an overseas population expresses its frustration with—or its admiration for—these countries, the executives and their products and services are much more accessible targets than ambassadors or political leaders. In other words, it is easier to firebomb a McDonald's than to attack an embassy.

The primary lesson for corporate leaders is clear then: business leaders, particularly those who oversee operations globally, can no longer be content to respect the traditional division of labor between political and corporate leadership. American and European corporations, many of which attained global stature in the 1990s, must recognize that they are on the front lines of American or European global influence. As a result, they, their facilities, and their brand reputation are vulnerable to anti-Western, antiglobalization demonstrations or operations overseas.

Consequently, corporations and executives must learn to become more holistic in how they view their businesses and risk within a social and even a diplomatic context. In practical terms, this can mean several things: business leaders must be more willing to spend their political capital educating political leaders about how foreign policies are sometimes perceived overseas, and business leaders must better appreciate how their brand can become a target for political activists.

This need is not temporary or merely associated with the war in Iraq or the war on terror; it reflects a permanent shift in how corporations must view their business going forward. It is a new reality of operating in a global marketplace.

IMAGINING THE UNIMAGINABLE

CASE STUDY C

A manufacturer with a long history of product innovation enjoyed steady growth until the telecommunications bubble burst in 2000. The firm had built up debt as it invested billions in new telecommunications technologies and company acquisitions, but no financial safety net had been created for what appeared to be the extremely unlikely possibility of an industry-wide demand crisis. When such a demand crisis did occur, the firm's share price plummeted by almost 50% in just two days.

Source: Deloitte Research USA, *Disarming the Value Killers: A Risk Management Study* (New York: Deloitte Development LLC, 2005), p. 6.

CASE STUDY D

In the early 1990s, a Mexican manufacturer used dollar debt from major U.S. banks to acquire plants in other Latin American countries and modernize operations. By the end of 1994, about three-quarters of the company's debt was in dollars, while the company's revenues were largely denominated by the peso. The company had not prepared for the unlikely event of a major currency devaluation coupled with an economic crisis. During the Mexican financial crisis of 1995, the devaluation of the peso and the resulting recession slashed cash flow from its Mexican operations by more than 50% in dollar terms. The company survived by arranging emergency financing.

Source: Deloitte Research USA, *Disarming the Value Killers: A Risk Management Study* (New York: Deloitte Development LLC, 2005), p. 6.

It is important to emphasize that although a risk may seem unlikely, its possible ultimate cost—the failure of the company—makes investing in preparation for the unimaginable eminently worthwhile.

Despite the potentially devastating impact of unlikely events, managers assessing a company's risk position often emphasize the most likely risks. Probability models, such as value-at-risk (VaR), are based on likelihood and impact data for given events. These models tend to be biased because they focus on the more frequent risks while overlooking low-probability events that can be devastating. For instance, the recent oil price hikes and the 9/11 attacks were events with a major impact on business that caught some companies unprepared. Such events cannot easily be classified into a probability model, and usually data are not available to model these risks.

Although "rare events"—from tsunamis to terrorist attacks—are not necessarily preventable, companies can adjust their operational and capital structures to better manage them. Stress tests and scenario planning provide an avenue for understanding the potential impact of rare events that are typically omitted in risk models. For example, a "stress test" examines a company's ability to withstand specific scenarios and events, without having to develop a statistical model for them. Stress tests are a crucial addition to VaR models because they help enable executives to answer the question "What can go terribly wrong?"

Scenarios for stress tests can, in certain circumstances, also have a historical foundation. In one such scenario, a company simulates market moves observed in a past crisis. Historical scenarios are helpful because all relationships between markets are specified at once. However, past market moves never repeat themselves in precisely the same fashion. That is why banks and brokerage firms often stress-test their portfolios and responses by considering a broad range of scenarios.

In addition to stress-testing responses to low-frequency events, companies need to enhance their capability to respond to chosen scenarios. A company can build its ability to respond to different scenarios by selectively investing in the requisite capabilities needed if the event occurs. For example, a firm might take a partial equity stake in a company in another market or region with the option to migrate to full ownership. Or a media company could simultaneously support many different technologies and strategies for online media distribution until standards become well defined. By initially supporting multiple technologies, the vendor in effect takes a "real option" to adapt quickly to future market conditions.

BUSINESS CONTINUITY PLANNING

The concept of business continuity planning has gained much visibility because of the 9/11 attacks, the proliferation of computer network viruses, and the occurrence of natural disasters ranging from hurricanes to tsunamis, as well as other risks. The ability to continue functioning after a major disruption is essential for companies that will be adversely or irreparably affected by downtime in their business operations.

Virtually everyone in the business universe agrees on the importance of enterprise risk management (ERM) and business continuity planning (BCP), but you're unlikely to find two people who agree on the definition of these terms. This much is certain, however: Although ERM and BCP have been around for at least a decade, they have taken on new meaning, importance, and complexity in the post-9/11 era.

THE PATH TO RISK INTELLIGENCE

Most companies apply some form of ERM, but only a small minority are what we might call risk-intelligent enterprises. Such organizations share several key characteristics:

- Risk management *practices* that encompass the entire business, transcending organizational silos and geographic boundaries
- *Strategies* that address the full spectrum of risks, including industry-specific, compliance, competitive, environmental, security, privacy, business continuity, strategic, reporting, and operational
- *Processes* that augment the conventional emphasis on probability by giving significant weight to vulnerability
- *Approaches* that do not consider only single events but also take into account risk scenarios and the interaction of multiple risks
- *Methodologies* that are infused into the corporate culture, so that strategy and decision making evolve out of a risk-informed process, instead of having risk considerations imposed after the fact (if at all)
- A *philosophy* that focuses not solely on avoiding risk but also on risks as a means to creating value

Recent research shows that business continuity programs are often not addressed at the enterprise level, and that companies frequently do not take into account dependency on third parties, such as vendors and suppliers. A case in point is the lack of readiness of companies in addressing the eventuality of an avian flu pandemic. (A fuller analysis appears in Chapter Six.)

The cost of imagining and managing low-frequency risk can be quite high, but the return on the investment is certainly worthwhile, especially in the eyes of a company's stakeholders. The return is undeniable, in the opinion of Joe Petro, who oversees Citigroup's security and antifraud workforce, numbering several thousand: "We have our own ROI. We monitor costs very carefully, and we constantly look for ways to save money. In some cases, the argument can be made that intelligent risk management pays for itself."[3]

A CULTURE ROOTED IN ETHICAL BEHAVIOR

CASE STUDY E

A major manufacturer was forced to recall millions of its products because of safety defects. With powerful financial incentives in place to meet production targets, workers had used questionable tactics to speed production, and managers had given inspections short shrift. The widespread problems with quality forced the firm to post hundreds of millions of dollars in losses in two quarters and drove net profits down almost 50%. The cost of the recall and expectations that sales would tumble knocked 45% off the firm's stock price within one month.

Source: Deloitte Research USA, *Disarming the Value Killers: A Risk Management Study* (New York: Deloitte Development LLC, 2005), p. 8.

CASE STUDY F

In just two days, a major health care firm saw its share price plunge by almost half and US$6 billion in market value evaporate. The company had looked like a highflier, but its extraordinary growth had come at the expense of an ethical corporate culture and solid controls. A variety of lawsuits filed against it had alleged fraudulent billing and other improprieties in government health programs, understaffing, and labor violations. When it was reported that changes in Medicare payment procedures would cut the company's revenues and that the federal government was investigating allegations of unnecessary surgery, its stock price took a nosedive.

Source: Deloitte Research USA, *Disarming the Value Killers: A Risk Management Study* (New York: Deloitte Development LLC, 2005), p. 8.

Unless a company has built an ethical corporate culture and effective controls, aggressive strategies to generate profits or slash costs can motivate employees to engage in fraudulent and inappropriate business activities. These practices increase a firm's exposure to operational and financial risks, which can severely damage its reputation and brand.

A permissive corporate culture and lax control systems contributed to many high-profile value losses during the past decade. In 2003, a study of major corporate governance failures and frauds found that the most common transgressions were related to overstating net profits.[4] Firms used a variety of fraudulent accounting strategies affecting revenues, expenses, and special reserve accounts. In the worst cases, a significant number of senior company executives were alleged to have openly tapped company funds for their personal benefit, profited from insider trading, or misled the public in their corporate disclosures.

Several structural changes have been legislated or adopted to improve control systems and processes (e.g., Sarbanes-Oxley in the United States, which calls for increased disclosures by public companies and improvement in their control environments). Another example is the Turnbull report in the United Kingdom. The U.S. Securities and Exchange Commission (SEC) and stock exchanges such as the New York Stock Exchange (NYSE) have also promulgated new governance and listing requirements. The increased attention to risk management by investors and the media has led many firms to upgrade their risk management and monitoring systems to guard against fraud and unethical business practices.

These legislative and structural initiatives will be effective, however, only if a firm has created a sound ethical culture. A corporate culture frames the shared beliefs of most members of an organization in terms of how they are expected to think, feel, and act as they conduct business each day. A firm's culture can often guide employees' behavior more consistently than formal rules can.

Setting or changing a firm's culture is a leadership activity that must start at the top. It requires senior management to consistently communicate—through actions even more than words—the ethics and values of the firm. These values should include dealing honestly with difficult situations by directly addressing bad news rather than avoiding it, sharing information, keeping commitments, and not overemphasizing the ends relative to the means.

One step to identifying potential cultural pitfalls is to appraise the current ethics and cultural environment. This can be done through a confidential survey administered to both management and rank-and-file employees. The survey provides an opportunity to compare opinions across different levels of the organization.

With the Sarbanes-Oxley Act requiring company management to file quarterly and annual reports on internal control over financial reporting and disclosure, management must take steps to reduce vulnerability to fraud. Beyond fostering a culture of ethical behavior, firms need to implement ethics programs that include written standards for conduct, training in ethics, advice lines, and the ability to report fraud anonymously. In addition, fraud detection programs that model different types of possible frauds and monitor the workplace to identify problems are essential to a comprehensive program. These steps can increase the reporting of fraud and help better manage risks before their costs spiral out of control.

TIMELY INFORMATION

CASE STUDY G

After a business service company disclosed that its second-quarter earnings would fall short of expectations, investors drove down its share price 37% and erased more than US$12 billion in its market value. Contributing to the losses was the firm's inability to offer much explanation as to what had gone wrong. After the turmoil, the CEO, CFO, and COO all left the firm.

Source: Deloitte Research USA, *Disarming the Value Killers: A Risk Management Study* (New York: Deloitte Development LLC, 2005), p. 9.

CASE STUDY H

A major energy company based in the United States slashed its profit outlook because of low power prices and fierce competition, sending its stock tumbling by more than 25%. The company's CEO admitted that the firm didn't have a clear picture of the business situation. Owing to deficiencies in its planning and budgeting systems, the company lacked the data that could have given it an early warning about the pending situation.

Source: Deloitte Research USA, *Disarming the Value Killers: A Risk Management Study* (New York: Deloitte Development LLC, 2005), p. 9.

Failures in risk management were often compounded by a lack of timely information for senior executives and boards of directors on the causes, financial impact, and possible resolution of the problem. This naturally reflects poorly on the senior executive team and its control of the organization, often leading to the departure of the team's members. The shock felt by investors who suddenly learn about the existence or severity of problems that had previously been undisclosed has often driven share values down even farther.

With CEOs and CFOs of U.S. public companies having to attest to the accuracy of financial information to comply with Sarbanes-Oxley requirements, some companies have improved the ability of their information systems to provide more current visibility into their operations. However, this increased knowledge does not necessarily translate into useful information for the board of directors. Board members are inundated with ever-larger amounts and kinds of information provided by management just before meetings. As boards of directors confront more complex governance tasks in a more uncertain and demanding environment, firms will have to redesign the way they gather, analyze, and present information to allow board members to discharge their responsibilities. Boards are increasingly likely to demand investments in information systems and staffs so they can independently monitor and assess management initiatives, performance, and company operations.

CEOs and corporate boards should take note: Those responsible for navigating their companies successfully into the future will have to rely on all relevant indicators of their company's success and risks—not just those reflected directly on the company's financial statements. But do they really evaluate the relevant risk management practices and performance measurements? Two global surveys of company directors and senior managers published by Deloitte Touche Tohmatsu and the Economist Intelligence Unit, titled *In the Dark: What Boards and Executives Don't Know about the Health of Their Businesses* (2004) and *In the Dark: What Boards and Executives STILL Don't Know about the Health of Their Businesses* (2007), strongly suggest that the answer is no.

The findings of the *In the Dark* reports reveal a troubling disconnect. Boards are keenly focused on the short-term financial results that their companies must report to the public. Yet they are often curiously out of touch with or poorly informed about other important indicators of success and risk management.

The discrepancy is significant. According to the 2004 survey, 86% of respondents said that their companies were excellent or good at tracking financial results, which normally represent lagging indicators of past performance. But only 34% felt the same about their ability to monitor nonfinancial factors such as customers' satisfaction, product and service quality, operational performance, and employees' commitment, which can be leading indicators of future performance. By 2007, respondents had taken greater note of the need to address nonfinancial indicators. Eighty-three percent of respondents (87% at companies with US$ 1 billion or more in revenues) said that the market now increasingly emphasizes nonfinancial performance measures. Yet in 2007, only 29% of respondents described their company's ability to track nonfinancial performance as excellent or good. These numbers reflect specific challenges but also a pressing need to address the broad spectrum of risk management issues essential to corporate viability and long-term sustainability.

There are several reasons why boards and senior management often remain in the dark. There still remains a strong focus on rewarding top managers who deliver favorable financial results. While this goal is important, it can obscure the real and vital contributions that nonfinancial factors, including risk management, play in sustaining corporate profitability.

As both the 2004 and 2007 survey respondents overwhelmingly acknowledged, all key factors—financial and nonfinancial—affect profitability in the short term and long term. Outstanding quality, smooth operations, and strong commitment by employees help bring customers back for more. Conversely, inconsistent or poor quality, inefficient operations, uncommitted employees, and dissatisfied customers will ultimately have an adverse effect on financial performance.

The same can be said about other important drivers of success or risk, including integrity and risk culture, innovation, brand strength, business strategy, supply chains, alliances, and community relationships. Although financial statements may in time reflect the quality of some of these necessary business ingredients, too often weaknesses do not become apparent until the damage has already been done.

A further complication is the shortage of recognized measurement tools. Nonfinancial metrics, including risk management metrics, tend to be less developed than financial ones. Sometimes they can be soft and inexact. But even if no regulatory requirement compels companies to report such nonfinancial factors, the marketplace will demand answers when stakeholders are blindsided by poor performance, a scandal, or a foreign attack.

Survey respondents recognized both this issue and the responsibility of boards to address it. In 2004, 92% of the survey respondents expressed the belief that boards are responsible for monitoring both financial and nonfinancial measures of success. Furthermore, 82% said that their companies would be spurred to reassess how they monitor and measure nonfinancial performance if such a reassessment was demanded by the board. Those are dramatic and telling statistics. However, in both 2004 and 2007, despite the dissatisfaction with the quality of nonfinancial measurements, survey respondents noted that there were several impediments to the broader use and greater sophistication of nonfinancial performance metrics. These include:

- Underdeveloped tools
- Organizational skepticism relating to the value of these tools
- Unclear accountability for nonfinancial performance

- Lack of familiarity with these measures on the part of boards and management
- Time constraints
- Concern that such metrics might convey too much information to competitors.

It is noteworthy that 54% of respondents to the 2007 survey noted that a greater understanding of how to measure nonfinancial drivers would spur a reassessment of how their company measures and monitors performance.

To advance the quality of nonfinancial performance measurement, several courses of action can be drawn from the 2004 and 2007 studies. Companies should:

- Take the initiative and try to develop metrics for nonfinancial indicators that are relevant to their circumstances.
- Closely monitor all relevant drivers and metrics of performance and security and risk management.
- Make those drivers and metrics the business of the board—and ensure that management is responsible for them.
- Set specific financial and nonfinancial performance targets.
- Create better tools to monitor and measure nonfinancial performance and risk.
- Tie compensation to an array of success factors, not just financial results.

Imagining risk and managing risk are not tangential to ensuring sustainability. To effectively imagine and manage the many indicators of success and risk requires leadership on the part of boards, management, and stake-holders. Therefore, organizations need to continually and effectively adjust and align their strategy, operations, governance structure, and the way they make decisions, so they can be proactive in identifying and quickly adjusting to changing risks, and protecting what is central to the sustainability of their business. The new structure needs to be transparent enough and have the appropriate levels of control so the board and CEO can address the appropriate level of risks across the company within an effective time frame.

CONCLUSION

Many of the world's largest companies suffered tremendous losses in market value over the past ten years. Many of these losses were created largely by a failure to correctly anticipate, hedge against, and manage diverse risks. Today, risk management is a critical issue for CEOs and boards as regulatory authorities and exchanges promulgate new disclosure and listing requirements that require more explicit information on risks and the risk management practices of the firm. To help preserve value, companies need to go beyond risk management in silos to create an integrated, organization-wide risk management function. Firms adopting such a comprehensive approach to risk management will define an overall risk appetite and will model critical interdependencies among different types of risks. They will apply stress tests and invest in new capabilities to increase the organization's ability to withstand low-probability, high-impact risks.

Regulatory changes such as Sarbanes-Oxley and other similar legislation are leading to improvements in control and information systems, but businesses must move beyond simple compliance to invest in creating a culture that leads employees to act as stewards of corporate value. Finally, business processes and information systems are needed that will apprise senior management and the board of directors in nearly real time of risks, anticipated problems, and the suggested response. Although risk can never be eliminated, companies that move beyond traditional risk management to implement a more comprehensive approach to their control environment will be better placed to prevent, minimize, or recover from losses in shareholder value.

BALANCING INTERNAL AND EXTERNAL RISKS

In this interview, Mark Layton, Global Enterprise Risk Services Leader and Partner, Deloitte and Touche USA LLP, examines the internal and external risk factors that companies may need to address, especially as the nature of business becomes more global and interrelated.

WHAT ARE THE MOST IMPORTANT ENTERPRISE-WIDE RISKS COMPANIES FACE TODAY?

I think you can break risk down into some key categories: strategic, operational, financial, and external risk. The amount of risk a company faces in any of those categories depends on the industry it is in, as well as a host of other issues. We frequently find that companies tend to look at risk within their own four walls, ignoring external forces that can affect them as well. As a result, some companies, even those with effective risk management programs, fail to take a holistic approach to risk. They might overlook global financial trends, currency issues, supply-chain matters, and so on.

WHAT IS IT ABOUT THE GLOBAL NATURE OF TODAY'S BUSINESS ENVIRONMENT THAT CREATES SO MUCH MORE RISK?

Everything is coming at you in so many different ways. A larger number of competitors and industries are becoming increasingly interrelated. In olden days a bank wasn't influenced by brokerage companies, financial services organizations, or insurance companies. In today's environment, companies can be affected by industries that were never expected to be in the same business. In addition to effectively managing risk in a global economy, companies have to be capable of dealing with cultural, regulatory, tax, and governance differences. Thus a company needs to have the talent available to manage such diverse demands.

IN LIGHT OF THE INCREASED RISK LEVEL, HOW CAN COMPANIES ENHANCE THEIR FOCUS?

They need to raise risk issues to the level of the board of directors and incorporate the risk evaluation and assessment into the company's governance processes.

This would provide the board with an understanding of the company's broad-based risks and how they are being managed. It's not that risks are to be avoided, but that they need to be managed appropriately. The risk evaluation should consider influences from outside the organization. For example, what risks could affect a company's major supplier, and what impact would that have on the organization? All of these elements enter into the picture and must be dealt with on an ongoing basis.

Further, it depends on the company, but the level of risk has gotten more complex for everyone as business has become more global in nature. As companies continue to expand their global efforts and the need for real-time managerial information grows, the ramifications have become more immediate. These changes only underscore the need for continuous evaluation and improvement in a risk management process. You can't do it just one time anymore. It's something that has to be ingrained in the DNA of your corporate culture.

WHAT KINDS OF TOOLS AND CAPABILITIES DOES DELOITTE HAVE TO HELP COMPANIES ASSESS AND MANAGE THEIR RISKS?

From a capability perspective, you're really talking about the entire Deloitte organization. Because risk is inherent in every aspect of doing business, all Deloitte's competencies can be brought to bear in a holistic and proactive approach to assessing risk, quantifying risk, and coming up with managerial approaches.

WHAT ARE THE BIGGEST SECURITY RISKS?

The concept of security has a broad meaning in the marketplace, ranging from physical security and homeland security to information technology security. For example, people tend to think of information technology security only as it relates to external vulnerability. Deloitte Touche Tohmatsu recently did a study (see 2005 Global Security Survey) showing that although the focus is on managing external vulnerability, internal security threats are even greater. Regardless of the source, breaches in security can have a huge impact on the value of the market's perception of a company's brand.

Source: Balancing Internal and External Risks: An Interview with Mark Layton (New York: Deloitte Development LLC, 2006).

NOTES

1. The 9/11 Commission Report: Final Report of the National Commission on Terrorist Attacks upon the United States (New York: W.W. Norton & Co., 2004), "Executive Summary," p. 9.
2. Todd Datz, "Leaders by Example," *CSO Magazine*, June 2005. *http://www.csoonline.com/ read/060105/intro/html.*
3. Interview conducted on January 27, 2005.
4. Jorge Guerra, "The Sarbanes-Oxley Act and the Evolution of Corporate Governance," *The CPA Journal*, April 1, 2004, cited in Deloitte Research USA, "Disarming the Value Killers: A Risk Management Study" (New York: Deloitte Development LLC, 2005), p. 8.

3

THE CHIEF SECURITY OFFICER

Among the corporate leaders with whom I speak regularly, there is a consensus on two related points: (1) a new culture of security and risk management is clearly taking shape; and (2) this culture is transcending the silos and discrete functions of large organizations.

Creating a risk culture does not entail surrendering to fear and paranoia. Instead, a risk culture focuses on setting standards, whether they relate to accounting and internal control issues, security, or human resources. These standards are useful for two reasons: They provide needed guidelines for employees, and they are essential for setting clear goals against which risk management practices and performance can be measured and adjusted.

Central to the creation and sustained development of a culture of risk management is the chief security officer (CSO). Sixty-three percent of the companies participating in a survey by the Council on Competitiveness have a chief of security. At those companies, most CSOs hold the title of vice president, and 33% report directly to the CEO.[1]

Admittedly, there is no standardized job description for the position of chief security officer. How the CSO operates within a given corporate structure is dictated by historical norms, the company's specific business challenges, and the unique talent and capabilities of the individual holding this front-line assignment.

But regardless of the industry, the job specifications and the expectations that go with them have been changing dramatically over the last several years, the more so since 9/11. "I wouldn't join a corporation today if I didn't have direct access to the chairman and the executive leadership," said J. David Quilter, director of corporate security at NiSource, a natural-gas holding company. This arrangement hasn't always been the case. During his first stint as head of a security department, Quilter recalled in an interview with *Security Management* magazine, the position was outsourced to him, as it was to many security chiefs at the time: "You sat at your desk. You got a call when all the horses were gone and the barn was burned."[2]

No longer. In *CSO Magazine*'s survey of corporate security practices in 2005, 59% of the respondents reported that the senior management of their companies viewed the role of the CSO "as a strategic and permanent position," a sharp increase from the 17% who saw it that way a year earlier. Likewise in 2005, 48% of the respondents surveyed said they considered security essential to business rather than an overhead cost. Only 25% said this in 2004. And 71% of the CSOs polled said that over the preceding 12 months, their organization's leadership had placed an increased value on risk management.[3]

During my business career, I have witnessed a proliferation of C-level executive positions covering areas as wide-ranging as knowledge management, diversity, and even creative endeavors. But the emergence of the present-day CSO is nothing short of revolutionary. Evolving from their historic role as guardians of physical security, and, in all likelihood, from careers in police investigative work, the new CSOs command high six-figure salaries and have backgrounds that surprised me. Of those interviewed for this book, one had been in the U.S. Secret Service, where he protected presidents. Another was a former FBI agent who had been responsible for securing the perimeter at Ground Zero in the immediate aftermath of 9/11. Yet another had carried out sensitive assignments for the CIA.

BREAKING DOWN THE WALLS

Although a background in government work isn't an absolute prerequisite for the job, it certainly helps, as today's corporate CSO deals with many of the same challenges facing governmental agencies. One of the most pervasive is the silo mind-set that exists in many organizations, where physical security is viewed in isolation from the organization's strategy and objectives. Virtually all the CSOs interviewed grasped the importance of getting past these barriers and embracing what is often called a holistic approach to security. Yet while most organizations endorse this concept in principle, many have yet to put it into practice.

As Ray O'Hara, Tim Williams, and Karl Perman noted in a paper published by the American Society for Industrial Security in 2005,[4] "Under traditional risk management practices, companies have addressed potential threats to the organization by defining threats as either physical or IT-related. But such classifications often result in stand-alone security solutions without regard to their impact on the organization's threat profile as a whole." Happily, some companies have begun to recognize the weakness in that fragmented approach, the authors note. "They are, instead, integrating security across their enterprises. They have found that integrated security creates efficiencies by increasing communication, reducing redundancies, and clearly assigning responsibilities within the enterprise."[5] Nonetheless, the trend is clearly toward extending the agendas and capabilities of CSOs into new territory.

HOW SECURITY IS ORGANIZED

It's probably not much of an overstatement to say that before 9/11, security was largely an afterthought at most U.S. corporations. According to Joe Cantamessa, a former FBI special agent who now heads security for Dow Jones, security has historically been considered synonymous with perimeter control and physical protection.[6] "Usually, security fell somewhere within facilities and general services," he said. "It was a building function and considered sort of a necessary evil."

At Convergys, an outsourcing services company with more than 70,000 employees around the globe, the security function had resided within the human resources organization before 9/11. Now it reports to the general counsel. "Formerly, we had just two people handling security," the general counsel, William H. Hawkins, said.[7] "After 9/11, there were discussions about where we were as a company and where we saw ourselves going. We recognized that there was a critical need to upgrade the corporate security function."

Actually, a growing number of companies have placed the security function within the purview of the general counsel. Citigroup, one of the world's largest financial institutions and one of the world's universally recognized brands, employs a worldwide security and antifraud workforce numbering in the thousands. At its helm is Joseph Petro, who, earlier in his life, spent 23 years with the U.S. Secret Service, including a four-year stint guarding former president Ronald Reagan.

Petro knows how critical it is to avoid even the appearance of conflict of interest within a global organization like Citigroup, which has a vast complex of business units, each with its own strategy, objectives, and agenda. For that reason, security for the entire organization is managed centrally by his office in New York City, which reports to the general counsel.

"We have regional security units, certainly," he said. "But the entire operation is managed centrally. In that way, we're able to maintain our independence from the individual business groups, so that security professionals are not encumbered in any way in doing what they need to do. They operate with total impartiality, sort of like external auditors."

Not surprisingly, nowhere will you find greater sensitivity to security than among those companies that operate nuclear facilities. Mike Assante oversees the development of critical infrastructure programs and electric grid reliability strategy for Idaho National Laboratory.[8] Previously, he was CSO for American Electric Power (AEP). He joined AEP directly from the military and after numerous years helping Fortune 500 companies with their security. "AEP decided it wanted to bring all facets of security together under a CSO position," he recalled. "After 9/11, there was a real recognition that the landscape was changing drastically. We were receiving inquiries about homeland security from every corner of our customer base towns, municipalities, and states as well as public utility commissions. There was a lot of anxiety in the air and a lot of stress on the system. Meanwhile, the FBI and other security and law enforcement agencies were looking for people at AEP to interface with."

At AEP, Assante reported to a chief risk officer (CRO), who in turn is accountable to the chief financial officer (CFO). For an electric power company, that hierarchical approach appears to make eminently good sense. As Assante explained, the traditional role of a CRO would be to oversee the management of various types of financial risk, such as credit risk and market risk. "In AEP's case, the CRO, Scott Smith, was also responsible for insurance and for operations risk, and for communicating any risk-based requirements back to the decision makers at the top, as well as at the individual business units." In other words, AEP approaches risk management holistically.

"But security and information security posed a separate set of challenges," he went on. "The reason is that AEP, like a lot of companies in this field, had originally relied on a shared service organization. This was a support unit whose main function was to service internal customers and help them get projects done on budget and on schedule without necessarily being attentive to security matters." To address that situation, oversight of security was shifted to the CRO and CFO. "In that way, we approach security in concert with all other forms of risk, and we are able to maintain uniform governance across the company." This holistic approach, he said, "is much better."

PRESCRIPTION FOR SECURITY

The individuals interviewed for this book were, by and large, direct and forthcoming in their comments. The one individual who insisted on keeping the bulk of his comments off the record was the senior security officer of a major pharmaceutical company. His reticence was understandable, given the intense scrutiny that has been focused on this industry by such diverse overseers as the U.S. Congress, the Food and Drug Administration, and the Department of Homeland Security.

Like other corporate CSOs, this one reported to the general counsel and had direct access to both the chairman and the CEO. On the record, he stated that at his company security figured much more directly than ever before in top-level decision making. Senior management regularly sought out his opinion on how the company's employees and assets could be positioned so as to best protect them. And, as is the case with so many of his peers, both within the pharmaceutical industry and elsewhere, his advice was routinely sought on matters pertaining to outsourcing and entry into new markets.

He related the story of a meeting called by the head of information technology to discuss outsourcing IT functions to India. As it turned out, he wasn't invited; nor did any of the participants seem unduly concerned about security. But when the CSO showed up at the meeting uninvited to give his perspective, "everyone listened intently, and then shelved the outsourcing plans."

CSOs also have a key role to play in terms of understanding employees' concerns and attitudes and guiding the human resources professionals accordingly. After 9/11, anxiety at the CSO's pharmaceutical company was understandably heightened. One of the CSO's tasks was to help the HR director respond to employees who worked on high floors and were asking to be given parachutes.

IS THERE A SECURITY ROI?

Can a company's investment in security ever provide a monetary return? When many companies were spending significant sums on initiatives to improve quality in the 1980s, just as many resisted the trend. They were convinced—mistakenly, as things turned out—that the investment would never pay for itself. Today, many executives consider security investments a black hole. Is their skepticism also shortsighted?

Perhaps. At Convergys, Hawkins sees several potential areas of tangible return. "For one thing, investments in security help us attract employees," he said. Convergys, which recruits heavily from local populations in such countries as the Philippines, Thailand, and India, offers a secure facility and work environment. "Our ability to assure prospective hires of a well-lit parking lot, transportation to and from work, security cameras, and so forth makes a big difference," Hawkins said. Then there is what might be called the reputational ROI. When a company invests in creating a secure work area for its employees, word gets out, and that becomes a benefit the company can take to the bank.

"Convergys runs contact centers for its clients in various cities," Hawkins explained. "In Manila, for example, we and our competitors have call centers all over the city, and employees at different companies often compare working conditions. So if one company is willing to spend more than the others on systems and facilities to protect its workers, you can bet this gets noticed. If we install mylar film on our windows to prevent them from shattering and possibly injuring our employees, it gets noticed. So, does this translate into a payoff down the road? I think it does."

Clients, too, value a stable and secure operating environment, and therein lies a second potential return, especially for outsource businesses like Convergys, where network continuity is of vital importance to its markets.

"If you're a client, and your performance requirement is 99.9% uptime, customers want to know that you've taken the steps from a physical security standpoint to keep the network up and running, even under adverse conditions," Hawkins said. "Do that, and you've got a definite competitive advantage."

A third area of return is the reduced insurance costs associated with higher security. At Convergys, Hawkins said, "we've built a reputation for security and preparedness, and this has paid off not only in lower insurance premiums but in a greater number of insurers willing to write coverage for our facilities around the world, even in so-called hot spots."

It goes without saying that a concern for ROI is ingrained in the culture and mind-set of banking and investment companies. Yet I was struck by Joe Petro's statement that he runs security and investigations "like a business." As he put it, "We have our own ROI, we monitor costs very carefully, and we constantly look for ways to save money."

In fact, Citigroup began investing heavily in security and continuity planning years before 9/11, "at a time when not a lot of companies were doing that," Petro said. For example, Citigroup was one of the first major financial institutions to establish a backup trading area. The company's prescience saved millions of dollars and also yielded a substantial dividend in its credibility.

"Because we had made that investment, on both the security and business reconstitution sides, we were able to get back up and running very quickly after 9/11," he explained. "It became clear that we'd done the right thing, even if it seemed like a lot of money at the time. The companies that didn't do this suffered, and some of them still haven't fully recovered from 9/11."

EMERGING TECHNOLOGIES

As you would expect, technology figures centrally in the day-to-day work of the CSO, who is frequently called on to evaluate advanced, and typically expensive, new systems for addressing new threats from terrorists and from white-collar criminals.

"New technologies for security are coming up every day: biometrics, cameras, metal detectors, sniffers, and so forth," said Petro. "The state of the art is growing geometrically. In the next five years, there will probably be explosives sniffers at every door in every building in New York City. Maybe in every subway too."

While such technologies are increasingly deployed to prevent or at least minimize the impact of attacks by dirty bombs and hijacked aircraft, that is not their only application. Another area where Petro concentrates is fraud, particularly as it affects online banking, one of Citigroup's fastest-growing businesses.

An especially widespread and pernicious manifestation of fraud is "phishing": the mass transmission of phony e-mail alerts designed to capture personal information from unsuspecting recipients. A typical phishing message might appear under the letterhead of Citigroup or another banking institution and carry a message like this: "Please click on the link below, where you will be prompted to

provide us with information needed to update our records."
The link will take the victim to what appears to be a legitimate site, where the person will be asked for his account
number, PIN, and other proprietary information. "It's very
clever, and once the phishers have your information, they
can freely access your accounts," Petro said.

The issue of authentication has thus become a big one
for financial institutions. Banking customers are personally protected through various laws and policies, so "the
banks are the ones left holding the bag," Petro said.
"They're the ones with responsibility for building the
security systems and staying ahead of the bad guys."

Muddying the picture is a psychosociological factor:
Customers are often loath to admit that they've readily
given out sensitive information; they feel embarrassed
at having been so careless, and they worry that they
might be liable for the losses. Demographics, too, are
a complicating factor. "The generation now coming into
their twenties and thirties grew up with computers," said
Petro. "They're going to be good computer criminals."
In contrast, he said, his own generation and those who
are called on to do the current investigative work, are,
for the most part, less computer literate. "While things
are getting better, the criminals are many steps ahead."

WE HAVE MET THE ENEMY AND HE IS WHO, EXACTLY?

Terrorists, phishers, computer hackers, Muslim radicals,
Basque separatists, Aryan Nation types—who, exactly,
are the people we need to protect ourselves against?

Joe Petro of Citigroup echoed the sentiment of many of his colleagues when he confided that he wasn't sure who the enemy is. "If you look at it from a global perspective, obviously it's al-Qaeda," he said. "But for a company like Citigroup, which operates in 105 countries, the threat is harder to characterize. We're in Indonesia, the Philippines, and Colombia, where there are local insurgents." Petro noted that Citigroup has been subjected to bombing attacks by assailants as diverse as the November 17 group in Greece and Marxists in Argentina. "So the threat is varied, and we have to be thinking about all kinds of issues all over the world," he said. "New York has one set of threats—the big catastrophic bomb, a dirty bomb, or another airplane." In other jurisdictions, the threats come in different forms.

The pharmaceutical security official interviewed was especially concerned about domestic threats, such as those coming from groups protesting against animal research. This executive was aghast to find that the U.S. Department of Agriculture had published on its Web site the exact location where this company kept its research animals—a bizarre breach of the company's security.

If there is one certainty, it is that everything changed after 9/11. "In Greece, terrorists would set a bomb to go off at two in the morning, when no one would really be expected to be there," Petro observed. "You could tell they were making a statement and that they didn't want to really hurt people." But the world has taken an unexpected turn in the years since 9/11. "It's clear now that terrorists aren't just interested in making a statement," Petro said. "They're interested in killing people."

The rise of the CSO reflects a widely acknowledged view that we must ramp up our security efforts or expose ourselves to irreparable harm. But some of the dangers are seemingly beyond our control. Protecting one's brand and reputation calls for new skills and new ways to approach corporate responsibility and corporate diplomacy.

DELOITTE'S DON AINSLIE: THE POWER OF TEAMWORK

Few will dispute that the world is a different place from what it was before September 11, 2001, but things have changed radically even since 2004. Just ask the global security officer for Deloitte Touche Tohmatsu, Don Ainslie.

When a tsunami in the Indian Ocean brought widespread death and destruction in late December 2004, it took Ainslie and his crisis management team several days to locate all Deloitte personnel traveling in the area and identify who was missing or in need of aid. "We were working with some 25 different travel agencies, each with its own protocols," he recalled. "Pinpointing everyone's whereabouts was difficult and time consuming." Afterward, Ainslie's team implemented a Travel Locator that centralizes Deloitte personnel travel data for a number of member firms and can automate the process of finding—and, if necessary, aiding and evacuating—travelers in a crisis. "We learned a lot from the tsunami experience and applied it," he said. He added, "The team was highly effective and synchronized, even though it happened during the holiday season."

Ainslie joined Deloitte after a career that included stints as an airborne ranger in the U.S. Army, a counterterrorism specialist, and a consultant for U.S. government intelligence agencies for 12 years. "When I joined, management had a clear sense of what it needed to do and when, and acknowledged that corporate security was a top priority." These days, Ainslie's team works closely with the heads of human resources at Deloitte's member firms and with their risk, information technology, and legal services. It's a broad-based accountability arrangement that reflects the significance of his role in the global organization's risk management structure—and in Deloitte's ever-widening concept of what security means.

Ainslie's weekly global security briefing for senior management addresses trends and shifts in the economic and geopolitical landscape that could affect Deloitte member firm operations—or those of their clients. His team has also established formal travel protocols, providing advisories to business travelers on "countries of concern." If Deloitte consultants are planning a trip to a high-risk country, "we make sure we have their itinerary and that they're equipped with a wallet card that has every conceivable contact number they might need in case Deloitte needs to locate them and pull them out quickly," he said.

"People play the major role in this business. In many ways they are more important than systems and software, which is how it should be," he said. One weekend a few years back, Ainslie was awakened around midnight by a colleague calling him from Philadelphia. "He'd just seen a news item on CNN about a fire in Madrid," he said. "It was the building of the Deloitte member firm there." By then our global CEO had already received a call from the CEO of our Spanish member firm, and the communications chain kicked in. In no time, the team had the ball rolling."

These days, Ainslie has his eye on a range of security threats that seem to grow more compelling by the year—avian influenza, global warming, cybertheft, and, of course, terrorism. "We try to stay on top of every possible situation," he said. "But we look at corporate security in football terms: No matter how well we're doing overall, we're only as good as our last game."

Source: Interviews conducted on August 16, 2004 and June 6, 2006.

NOTES

1. Council on Competitiveness, press release, "U.S. Private Sector Does Not Believe It Is a Target for Terrorism," October 3, 2002. *http://www.compete.org/newsroom/readnews.asp?id=94.*

2. Security Management Online, Sherry L. Harowitz, "The Very Model of a Modern CSO," April 2005. *http://www.securitymanagement.com/library/001727.html.*

3. Todd Datz, "Leaders by Example, in *CSO Magazine*, June 2005. *http://www.csoonline.com/read/060105/intro. html*.

4. Ray O'Hara, Tim Williams, and Karl Perman, "On a Mission to Merge," *Security Management Magazine*, July 2005, vol. 6, p. 1. *http://www.isaca.org/Content/Content Groups/Journal1/20058/On_a_Mission_to_Merge_em_ (JOnline)_em_1.htm*.

5. Ibid.

6. Interview conducted on November 9, 2004.

7. Interview conducted on December 8, 2004.

8. Interview conducted on December 8, 2004.

PART TWO

THE CHALLENGES OF GLOBALIZATION

As we are all aware, there are many serious risks facing the global economy. These include the continued threat of a large-scale terrorist attack, a possible avian flu pandemic, military conflict in the Middle East, and dramatic changes in the political climate in certain countries. To these, we must add the more predictable risks such as the eventual unwinding of the huge U.S. current account deficit and its impact on asset prices, continued movements in the already high price of oil, and the way major countries deal with demographic changes.

These risks are compounded further as the world economy continues to move—however uneasily—along the path of globalization. As a study by the International Monetary Fund pointed out several years ago, globalization simply means that world trade and financial markets are becoming ever more integrated.[1] Or as Tom Friedman of the *New York Times* has explained, "The world is getting flatter."[2] This heightened integration is creating a stream of challenges and opportunities for corporations big and small. While most continue to deal with these issues successfully, from my vantage point, all global and large national businesses also must confront the integration of developing countries, in particular China and India, and the affect their conduct—both political and economic—will have on the future of globalization.

The following section addresses these issues in more detail, but let's first consider some background. In Asia, per capita incomes have been moving quickly toward levels of the industrial countries since 1970, albeit sporadically, but a larger number of developing countries have made only limited progress. In fact, some have fallen farther behind. Despite this, it is fair to say that in general, the developing countries that are performing the best are those in which trade has grown significantly. Here are some useful statistics culled by Richard W. Fisher for Yale Global[3]:

- Trade as a percentage of gross world product has risen from 15% in 1986 to nearly 27% today.
- In 20 years, the stock of foreign direct investment assets as a percentage of gross world product has almost quadrupled.
- More people than ever are crossing national borders—for business and pleasure. On average in 1950, countries received just one foreign visitor for every 100 people. By the mid-1980s there were six. Today that number has doubled to 12.
- Since 1991, international telephone traffic has more than tripled. The number of cell phone subscribers

has grown from virtually zero to 1.8 billion—30% of the world population—and the number of Internet users has exceeded 1 billion.

There are many new realities associated with globalization that present both new opportunities and new risks. Some of these will be addressed in the following chapters. For companies that are navigating this business environment, the challenge continues to be how to minimize the risk from uncontrollable events while still taking appropriate business risks—noting that not all risks can be hedged. Companies must make informed decisions, and at the same time, they must diversify risk by making a complex series of bets, sometimes contradictory ones. This is not a new practice, but one that has been made more complex as we ride the wave of globalization that shows no signs of slowing in our lifetime.

NOTES

1. Eswar S. Prasad, Kenneth Rogoff, Shang-Jin Wei, and M. Ayan Kose, "Effects of Financial Globalization on Developing Countries: Some Empirical Evidence," *IMF Occasional Papers*, #220, September 9, 2003.

2. Thomas L. Freidman, *The World is Flat: A Brief History of the Twenty-First Century* (New York: Farrar, Strauss and Giroux, 2005).

3. Richard W. Fisher, "Globalization's Hidden Benefits," *Yale Global*, July 4, 2006. *http://yaleglobal.yale.edu/display.article?id=7670.*

4

OPPORTUNITY AND RISK: CHINA AND INDIA IN COMPARATIVE AND HISTORICAL PERSPECTIVE

Several years ago, the noted Harvard economic historian David Landes wrote a book, *The Wealth and Poverty of Nations,* addressing a host of important and challenging questions.[1] Landes began with some basic questions: How and why did Europe and the New World embark on a course of economic development that was radically different from, say, the Ottoman Middle East, Mogul India, or Ming China? And why was Europe so successful that in time, especially in the 19th and 20th centuries, it came to dominate other regions of the world both economically and politically?

In his careful analysis, Landes provides a provocative and detailed reply to that question. His answer need not detain us here. I mention Landes's study only because, to my mind, today we are at an economic crossroads—just as the world was in the late 16th century. But there is one big difference. Then, Europe and the New World would take a path that diverged significantly from the rest of the world. Today, the world economy is on a converging path. Domination by the United States and Europe will eventually end. New powers and players will emerge and converge to offer new opportunities and new risks.

We are entering a period of economic competition in which partners and rivals will be more evenly matched. We are also witnessing unprecedented global economic cooperation, whether you weigh the significance of the World Trade Organization or the economic power of the newly expanded European Union.

We are also, despite a potential global economic slow-down, in a longer cycle of major economic growth; a growth cycle that has transformed the economies of the old "first world" from manufacturing to service. Today, for example, more than 70% of the United States GDP is generated by the service sector. Similarly, the former "developing world" is being transformed into countries powered by a new mix of agriculture, manufacturing, and services.[2]

To any alert observer, it is clear that these historic events are having a major impact not only on the P&L of business but also on the way we manage risk and the very way we do business. Twenty years ago, companies paid little attention to the global dimensions and environment of business. CEOs of global corporations rarely ventured beyond the established capitals of finance and business: New York, London, and Tokyo. Now, it seems they are constantly beating a path to new economic centers like Shanghai and Mumbai.

The emerging economies of China and India offer a wealth of opportunities, but also new risks affecting not only the largest corporations but also many smaller ones that depend on Chinese and Indian vendors and service providers. I cannot provide a full analysis and risk survey in these pages. My intent is to select certain conditions, risks, and circumstances worthy of attention as India and China become major global economic powers and players in the next half century.

IMAGINING THE FUTURE

Let us begin by imagining that we are in 2050. The BRICs—Brazil, Russia, India, and China—have all emerged as significant players after following rigorous economic and fiscal policies for several decades. Here are a few conjectures or projections drawn from a very provocative study by Goldman Sachs:

- By 2050, the BRICs will have combined economies that are greater than the G6—the United States, Japan, Germany, France, Italy, and the United Kingdom. Currently, the BRICs are worth less than 15% of the G6.
- By 2025, the annual increase in spending of U.S. dollars by the BRICs could be twice that of the G6.
- As an engine of growth in demand and in spending power, the BRICs may become more important more quickly. Higher growth in these economies could offset the impact of aging populations

and slower growth in the traditionally advanced economies, including the G6.

Now for some more specific predictions:

- China's GDP will overtake
  - the United Kingdom by 2007
  - Germany by 2012
  - Japan by 2019
  - the United States by 2041
- India's GDP will overtake
  - Italy by 2017
  - France by 2023
  - Germany by 2027
  - Japan by 2032[3]

Let's consider China's and India's course of economic development to 2050 from a high level. Assuming that China continues to master the challenges of a hot economy, by 2020 growth rates will likely stabilize at around 5% from its current growth of approximately 10%. By the mid-2040s, as growth slows to a more comfortable 3.5%, confirmed strong investments rates, a large labor force, and steady convergence would make China the world's largest economy by 2041.

India, according to these projections, will continue to have a growth rate above 5% through 2050, while the growth rates of China, Russia, and Brazil could all fall significantly over the next 50 years. India's GDP will outstrip Japan's by 2032, and with a continuously growing population, India might well succeed in raising its per capita income in U.S. dollars to 35 times the current level.[4]

A BROAD OVERVIEW OF INDIA AND CHINA

What then are the relevant realities of today that we need to better appreciate as we seek to master the opportunities and risks of India and China?

Let me begin with a few broad points comparing India and China. India's economy benefited from a wave of deregulation and liberalization in the 1990s. As the world's largest democracy, India has succeeded in reducing the volatility of its economic performance while shifting average growth to a higher level. India's pattern of growth has, nevertheless, been quite different from that of the tigers of east Asia. Growth is not predicated on massive export manufacturing because the ports of India remain difficult to access. Nor has it been fueled by massive foreign direct investment as in China. But a word of caution is in order: Let us not make China the benchmark or preferred model of large economic growth.

India has done several things differently—but equally well. First, India is moving hundreds of millions of people out of agriculture into urban areas. Historically, this development has been critical to rapid economic growth more than once in Europe, beginning in the 16th century and again in the 19th century with the industrial revolution. Second, India's growth has been driven not by manufacturing in the way China has followed an accelerated industrial revolution model, but rather by the service sector. The growth in services has been the primary reason for the reduction of volatility in the Indian economy.

More recently, the service sector in India has shown itself to be a major export earner with competitive performance in several areas, including global outsourcing.

However, India does not have the option of neglecting the sectors more commonly associated with an industrial revolution. It must create a global export sector, because the pressures of the global market are irresistible. The particular weakness in India's exports appears to be in capital and in durable goods, where China and its white goods manufacturers, such as Haier and Lenovo, excel.

China, by comparison, has followed a more classical model of what might be called an accelerated industrial revolution. That means very high export-led growth. China drew on the expertise of overseas Chinese in manufacturing outsourcing and, in turn, leveraged cheaper labor and infrastructure at home. Much of the income generated by this growth was recycled to build up the infrastructure necessary to support the export sector—roads, ports, airports, and so on.

China's most important accomplishments have been in modernizing its infrastructure, enhancing the mobility of its labor force, focusing on becoming increasingly competitive, and attracting vast amounts of foreign direct investment (FDI). As a matter of fact, FDI flowing into China in 2006—anticipated at over US$60 billion—will be greater than total FDI in Russia between 1992 and 2000.[5] Since 1990, FDI in China has totaled more than US$500 billion, while in India FDI has accounted for less than one-tenth that amount. As for the 175 million or so Chinese workers who have migrated from the farms, they have found their way to the coast, taking jobs in industrial towns and complexes and living in dormitories.[6] They remit much of their earnings to their towns of origin in the interior, and this practice has helped drive economic growth. Competition in local markets has kept prices down and has allowed manufacturing wages to remain low and competitive. I should note, however, given my role in a global professional services organization, that wages in the service sector in China continue to rise at a much faster pace.

In broader terms, China represents a capitalist enigma—a hybrid of sorts, which one might call centrally dictated capitalism. The result is that capital formation is not driven by market forces but is instead a byproduct of old government processes and connections. Consequently, capital formation and allocation tend to be inefficient and often subject to corruption.

CHINA AND INDIA: COMPARATIVE ADVANTAGES

By all accounts, today China leads India in its command of global markets and its growth, but numbers—and there are too many to cite—do not tell the entire story. India's performance has been less spectacular than that of China, but it is worth remembering the fable about the tortoise and the hare. The tortoise eventually overtook the hare, and the moral was, "Slow and steady wins the race." If "slower than China but steady" is to be India's course, what comparative or relative advantages does India have over China?

Let's begin with a basic building block: human capital. China has instituted a rigorous primary and secondary school system and leads India two to one in the rate of children completing primary school (nearly 98%), but India has a significant lead in college and university education. In India, according to the IMD business school, 8% of Indians between the ages of 25 and 34 have some kind of tertiary education. Compare that with the United States, where 21% have some college education and 15.5% have a college degree. And India has one clear advantage over China: English is the language of instruction at India's institutions of higher learning. Finally, India produces 2.3 million bachelor's degrees per year and some 300,000 engineers.

In terms of having an education system appropriate for economic growth, India ranked 6th among 30 nations, while China ranked 25th. Regarding the availability of skilled labor, India ranks number one in the world in terms of qualified engineers. China ranks 29th. In fact, China is still not producing a sufficient number of university graduates. In 2004, China's institutions of higher learning accepted only about 4 million new students, up from about 1 million in 1996. Both foreign and domestic companies are competing for those college graduates. As a result, the cost of talented people in China is high. For example, according to Hewitt Associates, salaries for technical and professional staff in multinational corporations in China have increased more than 25% since 2001, whereas consumer prices rose only about 1.5%.[7]

Clearly, it is in India's best interest to continue to invest in education at home and abroad and ensure that it can continue to offer competitive opportunities and salaries for all of its graduates. India's challenge, however, is to create more job opportunities for the large portion of its population that is less well educated. Currently, about 44% of India's workers are illiterate. The challenge will be to create appropriate manufacturing jobs for them—the modern version of a challenge that faced Great Britain in the early 19th century.

A second advantage is the nature of India's commerce and commercial culture. I don't need to recite the history of Indian commerce, which has stretched from Asia to Africa and beyond, beginning with the commercial relations established with the Portuguese in the 16th century. India has a strong entrepreneurial spirit and strong commercial traditions.

Certainly, China leads India in its share of world exports of commercial services: 2.7% for China versus 1.8% for India. But the composition of those services highlights one of India's major strengths. In India's case, there is a heavy emphasis on scalable IT and software services. In fact, all IT-related services account for 47% of India's total services exports. An estimate by Morgan Stanley suggests that India's IT-related exports will almost double to US$50 billion by 2010, assuming that the current growth rate of 20% is maintained.[8] Compare that with China's current 13% growth rate. Again, these realities underscore the importance and the return on investment that English-language higher education brings to India as a comparative advantage over China in the decades ahead.[9]

A third advantage for India is the strong macroeconomic foundations of its growth. Since the 1980s, India's economy has averaged a 5.7% growth rate. The growth has resulted primarily from the government's strong shift in favor of the private sector. The result was a doubling of private corporate capital spending in the 1980s. Some of the benefits of this growth were offset by a balance-of-payments crisis. But a renewed commitment to economic liberalization, deregulation, and privatization has allowed India to emerge as a steadily growing player on the global stage.

SOME CHALLENGES AHEAD FOR CHINA AND INDIA

Now, what about some of the challenges ahead for China and India? Let me touch quickly on several issues for India. First, because India attracts a modest amount of FDI, it needs to concentrate on raising its savings rate to approach the average Asian rate of 35% of GDP. Currently, India's savings rate is around 24% of GDP.[10] Higher savings coupled with rigorous policies to attract further FDI and to reverse the government's revenue deficits could lead to increased investment rates.

Second, India, like many of the emerging economies, needs to recast its tax structure, especially indirect taxes and excise duties, to allow it to become more competitive with China. This will be especially important as India moves to enhance its manufacturing sector. The national value-added tax (VAT) implemented in 2005 has already removed some of the obstacles and inefficiencies created by the indirect tax system.

Third, India needs to invest in its infrastructure in a much more systematic way. Despite important improvements in telecom in the past four years, much more needs to be done to improve the electrical and transportation grids, including railroads and ports. According to one estimate, 60% of India's electricity distribution yields no revenues. Similar challenges exist for improving roads. China has seven times the paved road surface of India. Likewise, India's ports are inefficient. The lead time for India's trade with the United States is six to twelve weeks, compared with China's two to three weeks.[11]

Compared with those of India, China's challenges are more institutional in nature. The foremost issue continues to be China's banking system. The system is plagued by inefficiency, lack of transparency, and nonperforming loans (NPLs). The problem is that although the estimated amount of NPLs is set at about US$500 billion, the true value of the underlying assets supporting these loans remains unknown. Given that loans are often made for political reasons, in order to keep inefficient companies afloat, the assumption is that the value of the assets underlying the loans is fairly low. Nevertheless, today there are strong signs of improvement, and China's major banks are slowly going from the critical list to being in stable but guarded condition.

Second, China is a society of economic extremes, certainly more so than India. China's economy is being increasingly shaped by a prosperity gap between urban and rural residents and between the growing middle class (some 100 million people) and the rest of China's population. If the government fails to address some of the consequences of these gaps, China will have to deal with ever escalating rural demonstrations or uprisings.

The rural-urban gap in China is one of the fastest growing ever recorded in history, according to a number of world organizations, including the International Monetary Fund and the World Bank. About 65% of China's population lives in the countryside. And although many of the market-inhibiting or market-controlling mechanisms put in place by the communist regime have been removed, the 800 million Chinese living in the countryside have not benefited to the same extent as urban dwellers from the economic reforms and opportunities created since Deng Xiaoping launched the market reforms in 1978.[12]

Moreover, despite government intervention, urban unemployment is on the rise. According to the World Trade Organization (WTO), at least 40 million urban dwellers have lost their jobs since 2001, largely because of restructuring, downsizing, or the dismantling of state-owned enterprises.[13] Clearly, the social implications of China's transformation remain unknown and create a challenge of which the government is ever mindful.

CONCLUSION

Let me return to Professor Landes's discussion of the 16th century. His analysis contains one important and relevant message. In explaining the origins of Europe's economic take-off, he emphasizes three noneconomic fundamentals:

1. The growing autonomy of intellectual inquiry in Europe
2. The development of rigorous methods of intellectual argument that were shared across boundaries, despite language differences
3. What he calls the "invention of invention," the routinization of research and its diffusion[14]

To my mind, these values will be important as we look to the future. Intellectual autonomy and openness in democratic societies will continue to be important engines of economic growth. Shared ways of seeing and arguing about philosophy or business will be vital. As we look to the next several decades, we must find new ways to bridge the cultural gaps and differences that arise in the course of conducting business. To conduct business more efficiently, we need—here I paraphrase Landes's thinking—shared values and visions. Finally, we need to focus on innovation. The key to economic growth is not simply to improve on the ideas of others and be "fast followers" but to generate new ideas and new products. Those are some of the risks and opportunities that China and India afford us all.

NOTES

1. David S. Landes, *The Wealth and Poverty of Nations: Why Some Are Rich and Some Are Poor* (New York: W.W. Norton & Co., 1998).

2. For an original interpretation of the significance of the evolution from manufacturing to a services economy in the U.S. economy, see: Emmanuel Todd, *The Breakdown of the American Order: After the Empire*, translated by C. Jon Delogu (New York: Columbia University Press, 2003). *http://www.cia.gov/cia/publications/factbook/print/us.html*.

3. Dominic Wilson and Roopa Purushothaman "Dreaming with BRICS: The Path to 2050," Goldman Sachs, Global Economics Paper no: 99, October 1, 2003. Much of what follows is inspired or drawn from this bold and thought-provoking study. *http://www2.goldmansachs.com/insight/research/reports/report6.html*.

4. Ibid.

5. "Comment: Business Bashing Will Ruin Russia," *The Financial Times* (London), October 31, 2003.

6. Huang Ping and Zhan Shaohua, "Migrant Workers' Remittance and Rural Development in China"; Zai Liang and Hideki Morooka, "Internal Migration and Development, the Case of China," Social Science Research Council, November 2005 Workshop, "Migration and Development."

7. These and subsequent statistics are drawn from a variety of sources, including: Morgan Stanley Global, Daily Economic Comment, April 2, 2004; Jayant Sinha, "Checking India's Vital Signs"; and Emmanuel V. Pitsilis et al., "Checking China's Vital Signs," in *McKinsey Quarterly*, 2004.

8. Marianne Bray, "The New Faces of Outsourcing." *http://edition.cnn.com/2005/WORLD/asiapcf/09/14/india.eye.outsourcing/index.html*.

9. Institute of International Finance, Inc., "The Ascendance of China and India," in *Implications for Asia and the World Economy*. Ditchley Conference 2006: Selected Background Papers by the Staff of the IIF.

10. Geoff Hiscock, "India Looks to Accelerate Growth," October 6, 2004. *http://edition.cnn.com/2004/WORLD/asiapcf/08/31/india.eye.economy/index.html*.

11. Marianne Bray, "India and China: Rival or Fellow 'Tigers'?", October 25, 2005. *http://www.cnn.com/2005/WORLD/asiapcf/09/14/india.eye.china/index.html*.

12. Feng Jianhua, "Equal Education," December 10, 2006, *Beijing Review*. *http://www.bjreview.com.cn/ender/txt/2006-12/10/content_50384.htm*.

13. Joshua Levin, "China's Divisive Development: Growing Urban-Rural Inequality Bodes Trouble," in *Disease*, vol. 23.3, Fall 2001. *http://hir.harvard.edu/articles/977/*.

14. David S. Landes, *The Wealth and Poverty of Nations: Why Some Are Rich and Some Are Poor* (New York: W.W. Norton & Co., 1998), 201 pp.

5

REPUTATION AT RISK: MANAGING AMERICA'S BRAND AND IMAGE

In the weeks and months following 9/11, the world showered America with compassion and charitable concern. In fact, the French daily *Le Monde* proclaimed in an editorial, "We are all Americans!"[1] Since then, however, we seem to have squandered much of the emotional capital we gained on that day. The reputation of the American government and, by extension, that of everything American, including many iconic American brands, has suffered significant damage. Whereas a brand's American provenance was once an asset, now, in a significant number of cases, it is becoming a liability.

In the words of Keith Reinhard, chairman of the advertising giant DDB Needham, "Foreigners are transferring anger at the U.S. government to anger at the United States and anger at U.S. business."[2] If American brands slip far enough in the world's esteem, added Simon Anholt, author of *Brand America* at the Crossroads, "there is a chance that

American brands will one day have to work harder than others to downplay the negative associations of their country of origin. Or else, like so many brands from poor countries today, they might need to conceal their country of origin."[3]

Is such pessimism justified? Do American, and more generally Western, companies operating internationally really need to cast off their national identity—in essence, to unbrand themselves? After all, corporate America, despite adverse world opinion, is hardly a hobbled giant. According to a recent Interbrand study, 64 of the 100 most valuable global brands are still American-owned. Surely an American identity is still a marketable advantage.

Yet the signs of America's declining cachet are everywhere. Reinhard told of several restaurants in Hamburg, Germany, that have banned Coca-Cola and Marlboro cigarettes and announced that customers could no longer pay with American Express cards. In Scotland, the management consultant John McInally confided to reporters that he makes a point of not allowing his four-year-old son to drink Coca-Cola at birthday parties.

"I used to have a lot of respect for America; now there is mostly fear," he said. "You feel pretty powerless, but the one thing you can do is stop buying American products."[4]

BEVERAGES OF CHOICE

Boycott American-made fast food and fast cars because you don't like American foreign policy? That may seem like a stretch, but as Naseem Javed, CEO of the marketing firm ABC Namebank, told Clay Risen of *The New*

Republic, "People are asking whether a brand conforms to their ideologies. This has never happened on such a grand scale. But, post-9/11, it has exploded."[5]

Here is a case in point. Over the past two years, the Muslim world has seen a proliferation of "anti-Coke" alternatives, including Qibla Cola ("Liberate your taste") and Mecca Cola ("Don't drink stupid, drink committed"). Qibla's founder, Zahida Parveen, said that his brand "offers a real alternative for people concerned about the practices of some major western multinationals, which support causes that oppress Muslims. By choosing to boycott major brands, consumers are sending a powerful signal that the exploitation of Muslims cannot continue unchecked."[6] Tawfiq Mathlouthi, who created Mecca Cola, said that each bottle sold is "a little gesture against U.S. imperialism and foreign policy."[7]

One could argue that these are not trends but isolated instances of individual protest, but the evidence regarding American brands transcends the anecdotes:

- In 2003, a study by Research International (a subsidiary of the media giant WPP) found that Latin American consumers tended to talk anti-American but buy American. However, a follow-up study in 2004 found that their buying habits were beginning to match their views, especially among younger people in Argentina, Brazil, Chile, and Mexico.[8]
- Global Market Insite, which is based in Seattle, elicited foreign consumers' views of all things American. Eighty percent of its respondents said they distrusted the U.S. government, 50% said they

distrusted U.S. companies, and 39% distrusted Americans.[9]

- In a poll of European college graduates conducted by Edelman, a public relations firm in New York City, 66% of respondents in Germany and 64% of those in France said that, because of U.S. foreign policy, they were less likely to buy U.S. products.[10]

- According to *Newsweek*, an annual Roper survey begun in 1998 found no link between growing anti-Americanism and worldwide sales of major American brands until 2003. That year, Roper surveyed 30,000 consumers in 30 countries and found "that those who felt an increasing alienation from American culture were also likely to report a growing disinclination to eat at McDonald's or to buy Nike Shoes." The survey also found that "brand power" scores either stalled or fell for the top 12 multinational firms based in the United States. In contrast, 9 of the top 12 European and Asian firms had improving scores.[11]

- In a survey in 2004, Harris Interactive, a consulting group, found that only 7% of respondents in Britain, France, Germany, Italy, and Spain, all of which have a history of amity with the United States, viewed the U.S. government in positive terms.[12]

- According to a survey by the *Washington Post*, 100% of Egyptians—considered an important ally of the United States in the Middle East—feel negatively about the United States.[13]

THE ROOTS OF ANTI-AMERICANISM

The question that keeps recurring is, "Why do they hate us?" The conventional wisdom, especially in liberal circles, is that American adventurism in the Middle East has brought down the wrath of the world upon us. But, as Kurt Kuehn, senior vice president of worldwide sales and marketing for UPS, noted in a recent speech to the American Marketing Association, anti-American feeling was building long before the invasion of Iraq in 2003.

"Many in the world have also been upset for quite some time over what they perceive as an invasion of American culture and values," he said.[14] Anti-American feelings also owe much to America's rejection of the Kyoto environmental protocols, trade tariffs, resistance to the establishment of an International Court of Justice, and recent dealings with the United Nations. Still, the historical roots of anti-Americanism stretch farther back, to the postwar years, when the United States inherited much of the colonial baggage of Great Britain and France as their global power waned and the United States emerged as the principal opponent of the Soviet Union in the cold war.

Today, one thing is certain: anti-Americanism isn't the exclusive province of Islamic radicals or French McDonald's-phobes. The feeling is more widespread than we are perhaps ready to concede, and its impact on American brands is undeniable: "We are not speaking here of the frivolous grandstanding associated with temporary boycotts by a student minority," says John Quelch, professor at the Harvard Business School, in an interview with Sean Silverthorne, editor of *Working Knowledge for Business Leaders*, published by Harvard Business School. "We are witnessing the emergence of a consumer lifestyle with broad international appeal that is grounded in a rejection of American capitalism, foreign policy, and Brand America."[15]

Times were certainly better for American brands in those first heady years after the fall of the Berlin Wall and the demise of Soviet communism. Citizens in the former eastern bloc were drawn to American-made goods as talismanic symbols of freedom and free enterprise. But the good feeling didn't last.

In its current manifestation, anti-Americanism often takes the form of antiglobalization, and there is confusion between two distinct phenomena. "We suspect for many people the terms are synonymous," Kuehn said. "For some, 'globalization' is an American-led phenomenon designed to benefit the U.S. multinationals such as Coca-Cola, McDonald's, Ford, Nike, Microsoft, UPS, and others, which are widely seen as the symbols and promoters of globalization."[16]

Keith Reinhard of DDB suggested that there are in fact three root causes of rampant anti-Americanism. First, there are the exclusionary effects of globalization. "People in many countries feel left out," he said. "They feel they can never be part of, or enjoy the benefits of, the globalization movement led by U.S. business expansion." Second, there is the pervasiveness of American pop culture, leading many to think of America "as a criminally violent and sexually immoral nation." And finally, there are negative perceptions of the American personality. According to Reinhard, research from 130 countries "confirms that Americans are broadly perceived by others as arrogant, ignorant, lacking in humility, loud, and unwilling to listen."[17]

CREATING CHANGE THROUGH ACTIONS, NOT WORDS

In 2004, Reinhard formed a 150-member task force called Business for Diplomatic Action (BDA), drawn from the top echelons of the advertising and marketing professions. Its purpose was to "sensitize American companies and individuals to the rise of anti-Americanism in the world, and its implications."[18] It would do so by teaching Americans to modify their behavior, rather than by persuading foreigners to alter their perceptions. The BDA sponsored a far-reaching study of brand perceptions and also pumped money into the creation of a passport-size "World Citizens Guide" that would be distributed to American students going abroad to study.

In a sense, the BDA was a sequel to an earlier effort by the State Department to woo reluctant hearts and minds with feel-good advertising promoting the essential goodness of America and Americans. In 2002, branding pioneer Charlotte Beers was appointed "undersecretary for public diplomacy and public affairs," and was charged with boosting the American "brand" by promoting America's image in the Islamic world. When Beers resigned for reasons of health after two years, she was succeeded by Margaret Tutwiler, a former diplomat who in turn left a year later, frustrated by what she felt was inadequate support from Washington. She was succeeded by a former adviser to George W. Bush, Karen Hughes.

By and large, the effort by Beers, Tutwiler, and Hughes, which ran heavily to soft-sell television commercials, drew scathing reviews; the broad consensus was that the campaign was doomed by its own hubris. Its failure to produce substantive results "may have less to do with [its] flawed approach than with the fact that [it is] powerless to change the fundamentals of anti-Americanism," wrote Clay Risen in *The New Republic*.[19] And, in a white paper, the Council on Foreign Relations concurred: "'Spin' and manipulative public relations are not the answer. Public opinion cannot be cavalierly dismissed."[20]

But the council did not by any means rule out advertising as an engine of change. It has proposed that the United States launch a $1 billion, decade-long advertising campaign that would seek to accomplish what Beers and her successors attempted: to change negative perceptions of Americans abroad. "Attitudes toward America are marked by ambiguity and ambivalence, but they have become more negative in recent years," the council said. "This hostility is spilling over into negative attitudes toward American people and brands."[21]

Rather than blitz audiences with Pollyannaish ads about the goodness of America and American values, the council recommended a campaign that builds credibility among educated audiences by taking a less combative stance, "agreeing to disagree," listening to opposing viewpoints, and underscoring the ways in which assistance and dollars from the United States have led to major improvements in infrastructure.

In essence, what the council suggested is that if foreign nationals were informed about the United States' contributions to their quality of life—the power plants, roads, and water treatment plants built with American dollars—that would make a tangible difference in how America is perceived. Shelly Lazarus, CEO of Ogilvy Worldwide, put it this way: "If I were trying to influence public opinion, I'd do whatever I could to make sure that the people living in these countries understood that this power plant was brought to them courtesy of the United States."[22]

THE LIMITS AND POTENTIAL OF ADVERTISING

Are we in fact barking up the wrong tree in our determination to use advertising to tout the virtues of the American way of life and the benefits of democracy? Lazarus explained that "it's almost flattering when people think advertising can do as much as they think it does. Look, we went to war, people are being blown up. Do we really think we can just do some good advertising and it will take care of things?"

But others feel that advertising can be a potent force for managing and raising our image abroad. Among them is Allen Rosenshine, chairman of BBDO Worldwide. "It is wrong to dismiss branding as inappropriate just because it is mainly associated with commercial enterprises," he wrote in an article in *Advertising Age*. "On the contrary, branding precepts can be quite effective in persuading antagonists that our social, political, and economic systems are worthy of respect rather than contempt.

America is indeed a great country. But to communicate that to a contemptuous audience requires a carefully crafted message delivered with consistency and discipline. These are exactly the qualities that successful branding demands as well. At the end of the day, the usual critics notwithstanding, what makes us good at selling soap can help us sell America."[23]

The news isn't all bad. For one thing, smaller companies—those with little or no brand cachet—don't appear to have been affected. But while they may still conduct business-as-usual in their dealings with non-U.S. markets—enjoying a sort of reprieve—the day could come when the negative feeling directed against the mega-brands trickles down to the lower tiers. As Paul Grossman, international trade director of the Virginia Economic Development Partnership, put it, such companies "may never know what hit them; they'll just know they didn't get the contract."[24]

Technology companies too, even Microsoft and Intel, have thus far been largely immune from any kind of anti-American virus. The reason may be simply that people don't relate to technology on such intimate terms as they do to more mundane consumer products. "Cultural icons such as Coca-Cola, Disney, and Marlboro depend on emotional attachment rather than the cold logic of the silicon chip," says John Quelch of the Harvard Business School.[25]

One notable exception to this rule may be Procter & Gamble (P&G), whose headquarters are in Cincinnati. P&G is a consumer products behemoth and the quintessential American company. It's also the company that has written the book on globalization, with brands in virtually every country and dependency on the planet. Yet, unlike Coke, McDonald's, and other icons, P&G is a global company that has traded on its ability to blend in.

"Outside the United States, most consumers simply don't know that our brands are attached to an American parent," CFO Clayt Daley conceded.[26] "If we're selling Pampers or Pantene shampoo, most consumers in most countries don't know that those are Procter & Gamble brands." Or if they do know it, they may not realize that P&G is an American company. Contrast this studied anonymity with the situation of Coke or McDonald's, where company name and brand name are one and the same.

WHAT IS AN AMERICAN BRAND?

"There's no brand in the world that has Procter & Gamble as a brand name," said Daley. Is that a good thing? "In one sense it could be: It means we're less likely to have an issue on visibility." In the Middle East, people sometimes make a point of publicizing the fact that P&G brands are American brands; at one point, religious fundamentalists began spreading a hoax that P&G's leading detergent, Ariel, was named after the Prime Minister of Israel, Ariel Sharon. In the end, business considerations trumped ideology. "Egypt came to our support because that's where the soap was manufactured," recalls Daley.

In contrast, Asian consumers, especially those in Japan and China, "buy companies." Many Japanese believe that P&G is a Japanese company because it is common for Japanese companies to use Roman letter symbols to identify themselves, Daley said. Whether negative reactions to America's foreign policy are adversely affecting American brands is yet to be determined. But one thing is certain: Companies are not going out of the way to tout the fact that they're American.

Daley is not one to lose sleep over what others might feel is a loss of cachet for American brands. Still, he concedes that there are places where "being American" can cause problems, real or perceived. "I don't think we're at a disadvantage being known as a U.S. company," said Daley. But he noted that over the past 15 or 20 years, P&G has developed a significant non-American management cadre that, in these times, serves it particularly well.

"What the public sees is Procter & Gamble, and, yes, people probably know Procter & Gamble is an American company," he said. "But they're seeing people who aren't Americans interfacing with the government, with the community, and with the buying public." And that, he agrees, "may mitigate the impact" of America's uncertain image beyond its own shores.

In fact, several major U.S. multinationals have followed that same tack, rethinking traditional marketing, recruitment, and operational practices in light of an ever-increasing global presence. Starbucks, for example, makes a point of relating its products, store signage, and displays to local tastes and mores; Levi's has revamped its advertising to make it look less blatantly American than it did a generation ago. "Many of the big American brands have successfully localized themselves to the conditions of the countries where they operate," noted Mandy de Waal and Janice Spark, founding partners at Idea Engineers, a South African brand consulting firm. "The likes of KFC and Coca-Cola may be known to be American in origin, but they have done a good job of tailoring their products and advertising to [local] markets."[27]

HATE THE COUNTRY, LOVE THE BRANDS?

There is another reason for qualified optimism: Often the same studies that find rampant anti-Americanism, and a distrust of American brands reveal that people don't always practice what they preach, and that their buying habits sometimes run counter to their stated views. Lazarus conceded that, while there may be a certain amount of nervousness and anxiety about the American brand, especially in the Middle East, "at the end of the day, people may say things when they're surveyed, because they think it's the right thing to say," she told me. "But it may not really be affecting their behavior." Jan Lindemann, global director of brand valuation at Interbrand's London office, added, "There has been a short-term reaction against those with the strongest American identity, but the long-term trend is still very much in their favor. People in most markets still very much aspire to the American lifestyle."[28] But the downside is that stated opinions are typically a leading indicator. As Reinhard explained, "Sooner or later, anti-Americanism has got to be bad for business. In marketing, we know that changes in behavior inevitably follow changes in attitude."[29]

That said, U.S. brands clearly have their work cut out for them. The decline of the American brand may be merely cyclical. Shifts in the geopolitical landscape could, over time, turn things around. But how long will we have to wait? And will American brands completely regain the luster and global appeal they once enjoyed? Such questions don't really address a far more compelling set of challenges—one that transcends concerns about corporate security and branding. As we make our way through the first decade of the 21st century, how can we deal with a looming yet almost incalculable risk: avian flu?

NOTES

1. Jean-Marie Colombani, "Nous sommes tous Américains," *Le Monde*, September 13, 2001.

2. Dan Roberts and Gary Silverman, "Tarnished Image: Is the World Falling Out of Love with US Brands?" *Financial Times*, December 30, 2004.

3. Simon Anholt, "Brand America at the Crossroads," *Critical Eye*, Dec. 2004–Feb. 2005, p. 32.

4. Dan Roberts and Gary Silverman, "Tarnished Image: Is the World Falling Out of Love with US Brands?" *Financial Times*, December 30, 2004.

5. Clay Risen, "The Decline of Brand America: Remaindered," *The New Republic*, April 11, 2005. *https://ssl.tnr.com/p/docsub.mhtml?i=20050411&s=risen041105*.

6. "Qibla Taps Canada's Conscience," July 30, 2003. *http://www.beveragedaily.com/news/ng.asp?id=11974-qibla-taps-canada.*

7. John Henley and Jeevan Vasagar, "Think Muslim, Drink Muslim, Says New Rival of Coke," *The Guardian*, January 8, 2003.

8. Dan Roberts and Gary Silverman, "Tarnished Image: Is the World Falling Out of Love with US Brands?" *Financial Times*, December 30, 2004.

9. Dan Roberts and Gary Silverman, "US Policy Dents Brands' Reputation in Europe as Consumers Snub Products, *Financial Times*, Nov. 27, 2004.

10. Eric Pfanner, "Anti-American Ads Break Taboo over Politics," *International Herald Tribune*, January 19, 2004.

11. Jon D. Markham, "For American Brands, the World Turns Ugly," March 31, 2004. *http://moneycentral.msn.com/content/P76794.asp.*

12. "Countries Which Europeans Admire for Their Systems of Government, Quality of Life, Environment, Economies and Health Care Systems," Harris Interactive, June 29, 2004. *http://www.harrisinteractive.com/news/allnews bydate.asp?NewsID=820.*

13. Dafna Linzer, "Poll Shows Growing Arab Rancor at U.S.," *Washington Post*, July 23, 2004.

14. Kurt Kuehn, "Managing the Brand in an Age of Anti-Americanism," speech delivered to the American Marketing Association, Signature Luncheon, Atlanta, GA, September 8, 2004. *www.pressroom.ups.com/execforum/speeches/speech/0,1402,103,00.html.*

15. "Will American Brands Be a Casualty of War?," Q&A with John Quelch, in *Working Knowledge for Business*

Leaders, April 21, 2003. *http://hbswk.hbs.edu/item/3429.html*.

16. Kurt Kuehn, "Managing the Brand in an Age of Anti-Americanism," speech delivered to the American Marketing Association, Signature Luncheon, Atlanta, GA, September 8, 2004. *www.pressroom.ups.com/execforum/speeches/speech/0,1402,103,00.html*.

17. Keith Reinhard interview in "The Rebranding of America," in "East Meets West." *http://www.business fordiplomaticaction.org/news/articles/thebite.pdf*.

18. Ibid.

19. Clay Risen, "The Decline of Brand America: Remaindered," *The New Republic*, April 11, 2005. *https://ssl.tnr.com/p/docsub.mhtml?i=20050411&s=risen041105*.

20. Craig Charney and Nicole Yakatan, "A New Beginning: Strategies for a More Fruitful Dialogue with the Muslim World," *CSR*, no. 7, May 2005, Council on Foreign Relations. Accessed at: *http://www.cfr.org/content/publications/attachments/Anti-American_CSR.pdf*.

21. Ibid.

22. Interview conducted on July 7, 2005.

23. Allen Rosenshine, "Selling America to People Who Hate It," *Advertising Age*, February 18, 2002. *http://adage.com/abstract.php?article_id=33827*

24. Stephanie Stoughton, "Anti-American Sentiment May Hurt US Firms," October 13, 2005. *http://www.businessfordiplomaticaction.org/news/articles/ap_vcwt_oct05.doc*.

25. "Will American Brands Be a Casualty of War?," Q&A with John Quelch, in *Working Knowledge for Business Leaders*, April 21, 2003. *http://hbswk.hbs.edu/item/3429.html*.

26. Interview conducted on December 10, 2004.

27. Mandy de Waal and Janice Spark, "Brand America's Deteriorating Image Bad for Business." *http:// bizcommunity.com/Article/196/82/4607.html.*

28. "Wars and Boycotts, Both Fade Away," Newsmaker Q&A, *BusinessWeek*, April 8, 2003.

29. Keith Reinhard Interview in "The Rebranding of America," in "East Meets West." *http://www.business fordiplomaticaction.org/news/articles/thebite.pdf.*

6

IMAGINING THE UNIMAGINABLE: AVIAN FLU

Avian influenza caught the attention of world health authorities in 1997, when the first human infections of the H5N1 strain of the virus were reported in Hong Kong. In those early cases, the disease was passed exclusively from infected poultry to people, but there has since been a growing fear that the virus will eventually mutate to allow direct transmission among humans. If that happens, a global pandemic will almost certainly ensue.[1]

The specter of a worldwide avian flu outbreak has relevance for businesses of all types and for the service sector in particular. Deloitte is a case in point. On any given day, between 15,000 and 25,000 employees of Deloitte member firms are likely to be traveling, domestically or abroad. Apart from any health risks to which they might be exposed, quarantines, airport closures, and transportation system situations could strand them for weeks as refugees, creating nightmares on every continent.

But it isn't just the travelers who would be vulnerable. The flu virus has been shown to have a disproportionately serious impact on people 20 to 40 years old—that is, a disproportionate percentage of our workforce. No doubt the personnel of many other companies fit that same profile.

Some commentators have dismissed projections of a pandemic as just so much "flu hype," much in the manner of those who argue that fears about global warming are overblown. But consider this: Over the past 600 years, every century has seen at least three pandemics, affecting as much as 3% of the world's population. In 1918, a worldwide outbreak of Spanish influenza killed as many as 50 million people. The Asian flu epidemic in the late 1950s and the Hong Kong flu of 1968 also took millions of lives.[2]

What would a pandemic actually look like? Is there a way to characterize and quantify its likely impact on individuals and businesses? And, most important, is business adequately aware of the seriousness of the problem?

A DEADLY BOX SCORE

As I write this in 2006, avian influenza has infected poultry populations in more than 30 countries throughout Asia, Europe, the Middle East, and Africa. At the same time, the World Health Organization (WHO) has confirmed more than 250 cases of human infection, nearly half of them fatal. And now there have been several isolated cases of confirmed human-to-human transmission.[3]

Worst-case scenarios suggest that if the H5N1 virus reached pandemic proportions, it could spread across the globe within 60 days and remain active for several months before being brought under control. If past pandemics are a guide, an avian flu pandemic might come in waves of varying intensity, scope, and duration, some lasting as long as six weeks. Even conservative estimates such as those put out by WHO put the potential death toll at 2.4 million to 7 million. Others fear that as many as 350 million people could die.[4]

A full-blown avian influenza pandemic would exceed any recent crisis the world has faced. In its report of 2006, "The Global Economic and Financial Impact of an Avian Flu Pandemic and the Role of the IMF," the International Monetary Fund (IMF) hedges its bets, noting that "global integration with rapid transport and mass communications may increase some risks, while better public health systems and drugs may act in the other direction."[5] Nonetheless, there appears to be broad agreement that a pandemic would have an impact on virtually every aspect of human activity:

- *Business.* Financial markets could be destabilized for an extended period. Borders could be closed, shutting down foreign trade.
- *Critical needs.* Supplies of food, water, power, and medications could shrink to dangerously low levels.
- *Health care.* The spread of disease and its secondary effects, including famine and dehydration, could overwhelm health care systems weakened by a lack of workers, hospital space, and vital medical supplies. All but the most essential medical services could be canceled.
- *Civil order.* Riots, looting, and crime could be rampant. Police and military forces, decimated by disease, might be unable to restore order.

- *World economy.* Service industries, including hospitality, transportation, and entertainment, would likely be hardest hit by a pandemic. Declines in asset prices could put the balance sheets of some financial institutions under stress, according to the IMF. The retail sector and housing markets and related industries could also be directly affected. A worldwide recession could well result.

As I noted, these are the possible consequences of a full pandemic, but even a moderate outbreak will wreak substantial damage. The Centers for Disease Control (CDC) tracks the spread of disease on a scale of one to six, with avian flu currently rated three. Following the outbreak of seven new cases in Indonesia in 2006, WHO was considering raising the category from three to four. That doesn't denote a pandemic, but certain governments have already stated that they will automatically close their borders if their rating goes to four. So a pandemic doesn't necessarily have to occur for there to be extremely serious consequences.

AN ELUSIVE CURE

Exacerbating the situation is the lack of a reliable pharmaceutical cure for avian influenza. To be sure, vaccines have been developed, but global production capacity is seriously limited and not likely to improve anytime soon. Some experts estimate that it could take three to five years to produce sufficient quantities of a vaccine once a pandemic virus strain is identified.

When they're effective, vaccines keep us from getting sick in the first place; medications help us get better once we're infected. Antiviral medications do exist. Tamiflu is the best-known one, but recent events have called into question its effectiveness in treating influenza. In any event, supplies of Tamiflu would be barely adequate for even a minor outbreak. The CDC has stockpiled barely enough Tamiflu to treat approximately 5.5 million adults. That represents only a tiny fraction of the U.S. population, which now numbers 300 million.

"Don't count on vaccines to get us out of this, at least in our current state," said Michael T. Osterholm, who is director of the Center for Infectious Disease Research and Policy, the associate director of the Department of Homeland Security's National Center for Food Protection and Defense, and a professor at the University of Minnesota's School of Public Health. "Indeed, it's likely that little or no vaccine at all will be available in the first six to eight months of a pandemic," he added.[6]

Nor is the U.S. system of emergency medical care even minimally prepared for any sort of widespread health crisis such as a pandemic, a bioterrorist attack, or a natural disaster, according to reports issued by the Institute of Medicine (IOM). The system, says the IOM, "is overburdened, underfunded, and too fragmented to communicate and cooperate effectively across levels and geographic areas."[7] Surge capacity and the training of ER staffs are inadequate to deal with a nationwide disaster.

THE IMPACT ON BUSINESS

Strangely, there has been relatively little public discussion about the likely effect of a pandemic on business and commerce. A widespread flu outbreak would have the potential to cripple supply chains, decimate labor pools, and greatly diminish the ability of trading partners to meet scheduled obligations. Apart from the devastating impact on the U.S. economy, there would be a significant likelihood of large-scale disruptions in daily routines for families, companies, and society as a whole. Absenteeism among workers would soar.

Alex Azar, deputy secretary of the U.S. Department of Health and Human Services, projected that four out of every ten workers might be sidelined if the virus reaches pandemic proportions.[8] That estimate includes stricken workers as well as those who stay home to care for infected family members, look after their children in the event of school closings, or are placed in quarantine. "The absenteeism rate will include everyone, including your leadership," noted Kelly Donaghy, security and fire protection spokeswoman for Boeing in Costa Mesa, California.[9]

"A QUESTION NOT OF IF BUT WHEN"

I'm aware that these concerns are reminiscent of the fevered speculations about a global Y2K meltdown. But there are some compelling differences.

"It looked to the world as though nothing happened," said Steve Ross, who heads Deloitte's business continuity management practice.[10] "And nothing did happen, but only because millions, probably billions, of man-hours were spent preparing." With Y2K, he added, "we didn't know what would happen, but we knew exactly when. Now, when we talk about a pandemic, we have a pretty good idea of what's going to happen, but we have no sense of the timing. But everyone who I speak to agrees that it's a question of when not if."

To put a flu pandemic in perspective, consider the outbreak of Severe Acute Respiratory Syndrome (SARS) in 2003. In the greater scheme of things, SARS was a relatively minor event: only 8,078 cases were reported worldwide, and only 775 people died. Yet SARS virtually shut down the city of Toronto for several weeks and cost the Canadian economy more than $1 billion. Asia-Pacific's losses topped $40 billion.[11]

According to Dr. Sherry Cooper, a global economic strategist with Harris Bank and BMO Financial Group, even a moderate pandemic could cause the global economy a $1.1 trillion loss in the first three months, with America's share exceeding $220 billion. A more serious pandemic, she estimates, could cause a $3.2 trillion loss worldwide, $670 billion in the United States alone.[12]

It doesn't help that global supply chains are routinely managed on a just-in-time basis, with its emphasis on reduced lead times and zero to minimal inventory. "Just-in-time is a great concept, but it doesn't work in a pandemic," says Tommy G. Thompson, the former head of the U.S. Department of Health and Human Services, who now heads Deloitte & Touche U.S.A. LLP's Center for Health Solutions. "It makes supply chains all too vulnerable."

HEADS IN THE CORPORATE SAND?

Yet in many circles, the threat of a pandemic still seems remote and not terribly compelling. While most businesses have established plans to deal with natural disasters, terrorist attacks, and cybertheft, few have done anything to prepare for a pandemic. As Robert S. Wilkerson, a preparedness expert at Kroll Inc. noted, "If you take the Centers for Disease Control's worst-case scenario of millions infected and hundreds of thousands of deaths in the U.S. alone, corporations are just beginning to wrestle with it."[13]

In late 2005, the Deloitte & Touche U.S.A. LLP's Center for Health Solutions teamed up with the ERISA Industry Committee to survey large U.S. companies on their level of planning, preparedness, and response capabilities with regard to a flu pandemic.[14] The respondents' remarks were candid and, by and large, disconcerting.

Many of the executives surveyed readily acknowledged that avian flu is a potential threat to the United States in general. Yet, paradoxically, they seemed disinclined to view it as a direct threat to their own companies. Indeed, 60% of those surveyed said they were unsure whether avian flu posed a threat to their business at all or, if it did, they expected that the threat would be negligible.

It's hardly surprising, then, that only 14% of the respondents believed that their company had adequately planned to protect itself from the effects of an influenza pandemic. While some companies had begun putting teams or officials in charge of avian flu planning, one-third of the executives in the survey said that no one had been placed in charge. Perhaps most troubling, a significant portion of the respondents (39%) believed that even with planning, there isn't much a company can do to protect itself from the impact of avian flu.

What the survey results boil down to is that many businesses are taking what I would consider a highly risky wait-and-see attitude toward planning simply because the direct threat to business still seems unclear. However, many executives who recognized a direct threat admitted that their company was ill prepared.

CONFIRMING THE PREPAREDNESS GAP

Other surveys confirm what Deloitte & Touche U.S.A. LLP's found. Nearly 75% of the multinational corporations canvassed by *Continuity Central*, a newsletter in the United Kingdom, admitted that they had made no preparations for an epidemic;[15] in a study by the international HR consulting firm Watson Wyatt, only 15% of U.S. companies reported having flu-related contingency plans in place.[16] *BusinessWeek* polled six U.S. electric utilities and found that none has a specific plan to maintain power supplies in the face of a flu outbreak.[17]

As the world shrinks and national boundaries blur, international supply chains are more vulnerable than ever to disruption, and the consequences of disruption are frightening. As Sherry Cooper has noted, there are 70,000 multinational corporations worldwide and 690,000 foreign affiliates with almost $19 trillion in sales.[18]

The upshot is that we have a lot to lose. In a world where the global supply chain and real-time inventories determine almost everything we do, down to the food available for purchase in our grocery stores, one begins to understand the importance of advance planning. Yet currently, business is woefully ill prepared for even a moderate avian flu epidemic, which could have ripple effects across all parts of the U.S. economy.

To be sure, there are some notable exceptions:

- Intel has been using an electronic newsletter to communicate with its global workforce on flu-related issues and is reportedly prepared to relocate its manufacturing to countries that are unaffected.
- United Airlines has begun to educate crew members on hygiene and health-related concerns.
- Deutsche Bank has developed a crisis plan specifically for avian influenza. This plan includes moving employees from infected zones and considering possible economic impacts.
- ABN Amro, the Dutch-based global bank, recently created a task force to plan companywide strategy for dealing with a potential flu crisis. The group created plans to educate all employees about symptoms and appropriate responses and emphasized ethical considerations of stockpiling drugs in light of their current scarcity. The group also recommended setting up a task force team in each country

where the company operates, to monitor the health environment.

- Boeing has formed a pandemic planning team and is building on its existing disaster response plan to address the specific and unique implications of a pandemic. In fact, this aerospace giant already makes provisions for people to work from home in the event of an emergency, and it is now looking into the practicality of expanding the program in the event of a pandemic.[19]

RAISING AWARENESS

As a first step, business must be made more aware of the likelihood of an avian flu pandemic. Many of the business leaders taking part in Deloitte & Touche U.S.A. LLP's study seemed to be struggling to separate what they called "flu hype" from the scientific facts that could help them make informed decisions.

Government is in a strong position to provide accurate information and assistance. However, this information must be presented in a way that is credible and direct without being alarmist. Next, companies need help understanding how to plan; but first, many need to be convinced that planning can actually make a difference. As the Deloitte study shows, the challenge here is daunting.

Government can play an important role in providing guidance, best practices, and legislative relief relative to issues that might block planning. Unfortunately, Washington's track record in recent years has not inspired confidence. Speaking in 2005 at a conference organized by the Center for Disease Research and Policy, Tommy Thompson of Deloitte & Touche U.S.A. LLP cautioned businesses against depending too heavily on the federal government in time of crisis. "Instead," he urged, "reach out to your chamber of commerce, the National Guard, and public health officials."[20] Ultimately, companies must embrace planning on their own terms, deciding how they can specifically protect their employees, shareholders, and customers from the effects of avian flu.

Finally, business planning needs to extend far beyond expectations of access to a human avian flu vaccine, because the ability to produce such a remedy within the needed time frame is uncertain. Rather, companies, using information provided by government, should quickly begin identifying likely avian flu scenarios and developing ways they can effectively respond to these threats.

If the next pandemic is as bad as many public health experts are suggesting, it will be imperative for all components of U.S. society to do whatever is possible to be prepared. Business has a significant role to play in this preparedness. It's a role that we must begin addressing now.

DELOITTE: TAKING THE THREAT SERIOUSLY

No one can say with absolute certainty that the current strain of the avian influenza virus will trigger a global pandemic. What is certain, however, is that the world will face a viral pandemic at some point. In view of that unsettling reality, Deloitte has put a high priority on developing appropriate contingency plans.

Early in 2006, some 25 senior managers of Deloitte member firms took part in an Avian Influenza Global Summit in New York City. Its purpose was to build consensus on a proposed avian influenza response and to draft a set of recommended action steps. At the same time, the Deloitte member firms created a multidisciplinary avian flu "Tiger Team" to develop detailed guidance and tools to assist Deloitte member firms in implementing local preparedness and response plans.

Among the resources created to date are:

- *Avian Influenza Awareness Program.* An eLearning course designed to help all Deloitte member firm employees gain a clearer understanding of the current avian flu threat, share public health recommendations, and stay current on what Deloitte is doing to prepare.
- *Avian Influenza Human Resource Guidelines.* Recommended guidelines on human resources topics such as office closures, time off, benefits, and employee travel.
- *Avian Influenza Travel Preparedness Guidelines.* Recommended travel protocols for each threat level.
- *Hygiene and Safety Guidelines.* Guidance on member firm communications to their partners and employees concerning topics such as sanitation, food safety, social distancing, vaccines, virus diagnoses and treatment, and prevention.
- *Avian Influenza Communications Templates.* Sample communications that can be sent

> to member firm personnel about avian influenza at each stage of the virus.
>
> Predictions of a coming pandemic are too widespread and credible to ignore. But even if they fail to materialize, Deloitte's planning efforts have already enhanced its ability to deal with other major crises, including natural disasters, terrorism, and other global health emergencies.
>
> *Source:* PowerPoint Presentation, "Deloitte Avian Influenza Summit," New York, February 16, 2006.

Thorough planning and taking the initiative in managing risk does not always lead to predictable outcomes. Chapter Seven raises the issue of unintended consequences in the war on terrorism.

NOTES

1. For an overall perspective on the threat, see Michael T. Osterholm, "Preparing for the Next Pandemic," *Foreign Affairs*, July/August 2005. See also Laurie Garrett, "The Next Pandemic," loc. cit.
2. Ibid.
3. John Donnelly, "Pandemic Flu Would Outrun Vaccine, Global Health Officials Say," *Boston Globe*, October 24, 2006.
4. Tom Walsh, "Avian Flu: Preparing for a Pandemic," *Risk Alert*, Volume V, Issue 1, January 2006. *http://solutions. marsh.com/pandemic/documents/avianflu20051228.pdf*.

5. IMF Avian Flu Working Group, "The Global Economic and Financial Impact of an Avian Flu Pandemic and the Role of the IMF," February 28, 2006. Accessed at: *http:// www.imf.org/external/pubs/ft/afp/2006/eng/022806.pdf*.

6. Center for Infectious Disease Research and Policy (CIDRAP), 2006 Summit, February 14, 2006. Accessed at: *http://www.cidrap.umn.edu/cidrap/content/influenza/ biz-plan/news/feb1406summit.html;* cf. *http://birdflubook. com/a.php?id=28*.

7. Committee on the Future of Emergency Care in the United States, "Emergency Medical Services at the Cross roads," June 14, 2006. Quoted on *http://www.iom.edu/ CMS/3809/16107/35010.aspx*.

8. Alex M. Azar II, Deputy Secretary of Health and Human Services, "Pandemic Influenza: The Importance of Local Preparedness, speech delivered in Washington, DC, January 24, 2006. *http://www.hhs.gov/agencies/speech/ 2006/060124.html*.

9. Quoted in Nancy Hatch Woodward, "Pandemic: A Disease of Epic Proportions is Coming, Experts Say. Do You Know What to Expect?" *Society for Human Resource Management*, vol. 51, no. 5, May 2006. *http://www.shrm.org/ hrmagazine/articles/0506/0506cover.asp*.

10. Steve Ross, "The Convergence of Security and Business Continuity," CSI 33rd Annual Computer Security Conference and Exhibition, Orlando, FL, November 6, 2006. Conference proceedings on *https://www.cmpevents.com/ CSI33/a.asp?option=G&V=3&id=231450*.

11. CBC News Online, "The Economic Impact of SARS," July 8, 2003. *http://www.cbc.ca/news/background/sars/ economicmpact.html*.

12. Dr. Sherry Cooper, "Don't Fear Fear or Panic Panic: An Economist's View of Pandemic Flu," Special Report, October 11, 2005. *http://www.bmonesbittburns. com/economics/reports/20051011/dont_fear_fear.pdf*.

13. "Avian Flu: Business Thinks the Unthinkable," *Business-Week*, News & Analysis, November 28, 2005. *http:// www.businessweek.com/magazine/content/05_48/ b3961075.htm*.

14. Deloitte & Touche U.S.A. LLP, Center for Health Solutions, "Business Preparations for Pandemic Flu," Deloitte Development LLC, 2006.

15. *Continuity Central*, Pandemic Planning Survey Results, survey conducted October 6 to November 10, 2005. Accessed at: *http://www.continuitycentral.com/ feature0265.htm*.

16. Cited in "Few US Companies Ready for Bird Flu Outbreak," *USA Today*, May 1, 2006.

17. John Carey, "Avian Flu: Business Thinks the Unthinkable," *BusinessWeek*, News & Analysis, November 28, 2005. *http://www.businessweek.com/ magazine/content/05_48/b3961075.htm*.

18. Dr. Sherry Cooper, "Don't Fear Fear or Panic Panic: An Economist's View of Pandemic Flu," Special Report, October 11, 2005. *http://www.bmonesbittburns. com/economics/reports/20051011/dont_fear_fear.pdf*.

19. Gina Ruiz, "Business Continuity Plans for an Avian Flu Pandemic Largely off Workforce Radar," *Workforce Management*, Dec. 12, 2005, pp. 34-37. *http://www. workforce.com/section/02/feature/24/23/31/*; and John

Carey, "Avian Flu: Business Thinks the Unthinkable," *BusinessWeek*, News & Analysis, November 28, 2005. *http://www.businessweek.com/magazine/content/05_48/b3961075.htm*.

20. Deloitte Global Security Office, "Global Crisis Management Plan Pandemic Influenza: Avian Influenza Preparedness and Response Plan," October 2005; PowerPoint Presentation, "Deloitte Avian Influenza Summit," New York, February 16, 2006; Deloitte online eLearning course, "Avian Influenza: Understand, Plan, and Prepare."

7

AN UNINTENDED CONSEQUENCE: SECURITY, IMMIGRATION, AND EDUCATION

Whatever headway we may be making against al-Qaeda, the war on terror is having an unplanned consequence: it may be threatening to undermine U.S. business leadership by hampering the ability of U.S. universities and corporations to recruit and train foreign-born students, scientists, and engineers.

Apart from the damage it does to individual career aspirations, America's increasingly onerous visa and immigration policies "are costing us access to some of the best and brightest minds in the world," noted Dr. Frank Barnes, a professor of engineering at the University of Colorado at Boulder.[1] "One of the reasons we're a leader in, say, electronics—or have been—is because of many of the people who have come to the United States as immigrants, or come as students, and gone on to make major contributions."

Now, instead of coming to the United States to study physics at Princeton or petroleum engineering at Louisiana State, more foreign students are choosing universities in Sydney and London, Amsterdam, and Hamburg. Once accepted at overseas institutions of higher learning, the chances of their ever returning to the United States to live and work are minimal.

For one thing, the obstacles to legal entry are making many foreigners throw up their hands in despair. It's understandable. Rather than risk being caught up in a nightmare of red tape and administrative indifference before being allowed to study or work here, many are taking the path of least resistance and pursuing their careers in places they perceive as more welcoming.

HARD TO GET HERE, HARDER TO STAY

Those who do come to the United States may find it difficult to stay, as it can take upwards of two years to be granted permanent residency. The waiting period for an employment-based green card can be even longer. Those already in the United States are finding the going a lot tougher than they ever imagined it would be.

- At the University of Colorado at Boulder, a graduate student, Yijing Fu, is conducting research that could dramatically expand the bandwidth of fiber-optic lines and revolutionize the speed at which information is transmitted. In 2003, Yu returned home to China for a brief visit with his family, only to be barred from reentering the United

States because his visa had been sent to Washington for a special security review. It took six months for him to be allowed back into the United States, according to a PBS news report. This cost him and the university invaluable research time.[2]

- In 2003, according to a report by the American Immigration Law Foundation (AILF) Immigration Policy Center, the UCLA Medical Center lost a Pakistani pediatric heart surgeon for seven months while he was stranded abroad awaiting his visa. The doctor had 10 years of U.S. medical training but was subjected to a lengthy and "ultimately fruitless" investigation into his background, the report said.[3]

- The AILF reported the case of an Indonesian engineer who applied for a renewal of his L-1 visa after working in the United States. "The delay in processing his request led the company to transfer him to an overseas office, to move projects abroad in order to complete them," the AILF noted.[4]

- According to a report in the *Washington Post*, Dennis Eremin, a Russian physicist who had been teaching at the University of Texas at Austin for five years, returned to Russia to get married. It took the U.S. State Department 10 months to issue him a visa so that he could come back to the United States and complete his Ph.D. program.[5]

- The scientist George McMechan at the University of Texas at Dallas told the *Dallas Morning News* that eight Chinese doctoral students he'd recruited to work at the school's Center for Lithospheric Studies had been denied visas by Washington.[6] The researchers would have helped in the search for new oil reserves, McMechan said, "but, basically, some research projects are dying."

- The number of new international graduate students at American universities declined by 8% in 2002, 10% in 2003, and 3% in 2004, according to a recent report by the Council of Graduate Schools.[7] "Our national concerns for enhanced security may have had the unintended and untimely effect of tipping international demand in favor of our international competitors," the council noted.

What is doubly disconcerting about these stories is that they are not isolated glitches in an otherwise sound immigration policy. Rather, they are symptoms of a policy that is in serious need of basic reexamination and repair. Restrictive visa policies aren't the only thing discouraging international students from coming here. Other factors include "fierce competition for students with Britain, Japan, and other countries; improvements in the economies and universities of China and India, the countries that send the largest number of students here; the cost of an American education; and a perception that the United States is not interested in attracting international students," writes Stuart Anderson in the *New York Times*.[8]

According to the National Science Board, in the decade before 9/11, the proportion of foreign-born scientists and engineers in the United States rose from 24% to 38%. That percentage has declined every year since 9/11.[9]

THE CASE FOR VIGILANCE

Since 9/11 and, arguably, since much earlier, there has been a need for heightened security in issuing student visas. One of the plotters of the attack on the World Trade Center was in the United States on a student visa. "There has to be a balance between openness in the global scientific enterprise and protecting ourselves," said Jordan Konisky, vice provost for research and graduate studies at Rice University in Texas. "Obviously, we have to worry about this technology that's flowing back and forth across international borders. This threat—no one likes it. But we have to have some kind of reasonable response.[10]

It's a view that more and more academicians espouse these days. "Nobody denies the importance of barring entry to terrorists," noted the *New York Times* in an editorial in 2005. "But nobody should be oblivious to the danger of excluding another Einstein."[11]

The *Times*'s point is well-taken. A study in 2004 by the economist Keith Maskus of the University of Colorado and Gnanaraj Chellaraj and Aaditya Mattoo of the World Bank noted that every 100 foreign-born students who gain science or engineering doctorates from U.S. universities account for 62 patent applications. Thus "reductions in foreign graduate students from visa restrictions could significantly reduce U.S. innovative activity," the authors said.[12]

A study in 2005 by California's Bay Area Science and Innovation Consortium (BASIC) freely acknowledged that porous borders "make for weak security" and that "there is an indisputable need to screen for terrorists and track potential security risks."[13] But in its zeal to bar those who would harm us, the United States has stumbled into a "baby-and-bathwater" situation. As the BASIC study noted, "Foreign students and scientific colleagues have always been a key ingredient of innovation in the U.S. While the need for measured improvements in security is clear, we need to reevaluate our risk acceptance posture to make sure that needless measures do not damage our ability to compete as a nation."[14]

Dr. William Wulf, president of the National Academy of Engineering, is worried about the dwindling number of foreign graduate students and its implications for the future of scientific progress in the United States. "My father came to the United States from Germany, so, as a first-generation American, I suppose, I'm particularly attuned to issues related to immigration and immigration restrictions," he reflected.

"THE BACKBONE OF AMERICAN SCIENCE AND ENGINEERING"

Testifying before the House Judiciary Committee's Subcommittee on Immigration, Border Security, and Claims in 2005, Wulf noted that during the postwar era, many of America's foremost scientific figures came from Europe: "There are the famous names like Einstein, Fermi, and Teller (without whom we might not have been the first to build the atomic bomb), von Braun (without whom we would not be ascendant in rockets and space), and von Neumann (without whom we might not be leaders in computing and information technology)," he said. "But there are dozens more, like Bethe and Gödel, that may not be known to the general public, but who formed the backbone of American science and engineering plus an enormous number of journeymen scientists and engineers whose individual contributions will never be celebrated, but without whom the United States would be neither as prosperous nor as secure as it is."[15]

Today, it isn't just European names that dominate the roster of America's scientific leaders. Rather, Wulf told the subcommittee, "the names are like those of Praveen Chaudhary (now director of Brookhaven National Lab), Venkatesh Narayanamurti (dean of the Division of Engineering and Applied Sciences at Harvard), C. N. Yang (Nobel laureate physicist, from the Institute for Advanced Study in Princeton), Katepalli Sreenivasan (recent director of the Institute for Physical Science and Technology at the University of Maryland), and Elias Zerhouni (who was born in Algeria and now is the director of the National Institutes of Health)."[16]

DECLINING MBA APPLICATIONS

It will be evident that the scientific fields have been most directly affected by the United States' restrictions on immigration. As Allison Chamberlain noted in an article published by the American Association for the Advancement of Science, "Because students in the science and engineering fields are more likely to study one of the sensitive subjects on the government's Technology Alert

List, they are likely to face even greater security checks by the Visas Mantis." (Visas Mantis is a security clearance program aimed at preventing the illegal transfer of technology out of the United States.)[17]

In a study of 71 cases, the Government Accountability Office (GAO) found that it took more than two months, on average, to review applications requiring a more extensive Visas Mantis review. "With such long delays, students are becoming discouraged with coming to the United States, which may explain increases in foreign applicants for other countries," Chamberlain said. For example, Australia experienced a 16.5% increase in the number of foreign students in the academic year 2003.[18]

However, scientists and engineers are not the only ones affected. Business students have also begun to shy away from the United States. Since the early 1990s, talented foreign students have been highly sought after by multinational corporations based in the United States. But these days, there seem to be fewer of them to choose from. According to a recent study by the Graduate Management Admission Council, nearly three-quarters of the nation's MBA programs experienced a significant decline in international applications to their schools in 2003.[19]

"All the countries are looking over here—how you run the stock exchange, how you run your companies," Adolf Kristjansson, an MBA candidate studying at Old Dominion University in Virginia told the *Norfolk Virginian-Pilot*. But Kristjansson, who came to the United States from Iceland, was not sanguine about his future in this country. "Even if I had a good company that wanted me to work for them," he said, "there's no way to guarantee that I would get a visa to work in the United States."[20]

So instead of learning the workings of U.S. capitalism and a pluralistic society and instead of obtaining internships and executive training opportunities at Procter & Gamble and ExxonMobil, many European MBA candidates are bypassing U.S. universities altogether; those that do come here are increasingly likely to return home once they have completed their studies and go to work for European companies like Shell and Unilever.

THE IMPACT ON SCIENTIFIC CONFERENCES

Severe visa restrictions are hurting academic conferences as well. *The Scientist* reported that two Chinese-born students at the University of Toronto were barred from attending an environmental toxicology and chemistry conference in Austin, Texas, in November 2003, even though they had applied early for their visas, had booked all their travel plans, were invited to present research posters, and had attended the same meeting in 2002. "It took three months to process the security and background checks on the two well past the conference date," *The Scientist* noted.[21] A year earlier, an Iranian-born professor at the University of Toronto who was a Canadian citizen angrily withdrew from a National Science Foundation meeting after being fingerprinted, photographed, and subjected to intense scrutiny by U.S. immigration officials.[22]

The Russian Academy of Sciences represents the crème de la crème of Russian scholars. Even during the cold war, the conference figured importantly in a very active exchange of U.S. and Soviet scholars, Wulf noted. Indeed, he believes that these exchanges were absolutely crucial to the termination of the cold war. And now? Recently, Wulf explained now, Russian scholars from the Academy of Sciences were scheduled to attend a major academic conference in the United States but couldn't get the required visas. Wulf, who visited Russia during this time, remembered the turmoil and rage the situation caused.

"I wasn't prepared for the emotional strength of their response," he said. "You don't normally see these academics get angry. I was just blown away by their reaction—shaking fists, voices quavering." Wulf told the story about "some 25-year-old junior-level State Department official who made a senior scholar wait for more than a year to get his visa. To make matters worse, the embassy held his passport the whole time, so that he couldn't travel anywhere else."

BAD CAREER MOVES

A big part of the problem, Wulf explained, is that "a consular officer who grants a visa to someone who later commits a terrorist act in the United States may be subjected to department review and serious disciplinary action. But at the same time, there are no offsetting incentives for consular officers to serve the national interest by facilitating scientific exchanges." In other words, granting a visa can be a bad career move; that's why consular officials "often send visa applications back to the United States for sequential security clearances by several agencies, leading to long delays and backlogs," Wulf said. Frank Barnes of the University of Colorado put it even more bluntly: "If you're a clerk in the State Department and you let in a terrorist, you're in big trouble. But if a qualified student never makes it to the United States, you're never going to hear about it."

These situations are not unique or even unusual. As a result, more international scientific conferences are being held outside the United States, imposing higher costs on our scholars and inhibiting their participation in these important events.

What's more, foreign students are often prohibited from using certain "deemed exports" to perform their academic studies. The term refers to the ban on transferring certain technologies and technical data to foreign nationals working or studying in the United States. A professor of public affairs, Barry Bergman, writing in the *UCBerkeley News*, acknowledged that in an age when data can be dangerous, there is justification for "keeping classified information out of the hands of America's enemies, from terrorist networks to hostile regimes." But university officials "warn of a dimly grasped threat from the U.S. government itself," he said, "having less to do with legitimate security than with a needless clampdown on academic freedom including moves to bar non-citizens and even foreign-born U.S. citizens from participating in an ever-expanding list of science and engineering research projects."[23]

While the "deemed export" rules are often Byzantine and abstruse, they can be and have been applied to bar a foreign-born medical student in the United States from using certain types of high-powered microscopes or a mathematics student from using a high-performance computer. Violators face criminal penalties. Wulf concluded: "I guess this type of policy says, 'We have all the answers.' "

WEIGHING THE RISKS AND THE BENEFITS

Frank Barnes argues for discussion of the risks and rewards of such constraints. "We can't guarantee that a more liberal visa requirement wouldn't add some risk," he told me, "but this risk must be measured against the potential benefits." Has there been such an open dialogue? Not by a long shot. Wulf and Barnes agreed that there are no easy answers; what's needed, rather, is a fuller public discussion of the issues, including a dispassionate examination of the costs and benefits.

In a real sense, the continued education of foreign students is a short-term issue. The long-term problem is the potential loss of influence of American business in the global marketplace. The fact is that U.S. foreign policy and American business leadership have been integrally connected. During the Vietnam war, for example, it wasn't only the government that protesters railed against; the business community was also targeted.

But today new dynamics seem to be prevailing: the side-by-side globalization of business and terrorism. Are we in danger of commingling globalization with the war

on terror? Is our government's zest to root out terrorist threats and regimes being seen as an adjunct to the
worldwide growth of capitalism? Just as economic globalization isn't the product of a single country or group,
the spread of terrorism has multiple sources and agendas.

New dynamics are also at work in the amazing growth
of the European Union (EU). In a few years, this economic powerhouse will stretch from Ireland in the west to
Greece in the east and may come to include the 48 million
people of the Ukraine. If America's "go it alone" foreign
policy preoccupies our "blood and treasure," I believe it's
safe to assume that the EU will seize the opportunity to
cultivate new markets, providing economic alternatives
to U.S. companies and polishing its image as a viable
alternative to the U.S. hegemony.

William Wulf explained that while the United States
is putting in place restrictive and, some say, unfair visa
regulations for foreign students, other countries have lib-
eralized their visa laws to compete for these students.
Adolf Krisjansson noted that many nations in the EU are
beginning to offer the equivalent of "in-state-resident"
tuition discounts to all EU graduate students.[24] The EU
is also giving serious consideration "to offering citizen-
ship to foreign students who complete their doctorates at
European universities," the *New York Times* reported.[25]

The brain drain doesn't have to continue unabated;
any number of recommendations have been put forward
by various academic and scientific bodies for facilitating
the entry of international students and scientists without exposing the country to additional security risks.

As early as 2002, Wulf, together with the president of the National Academy of Sciences, Bruce Alberts, and Harvey Fineberg, president of the Institute of Medicine, issued a statement that suggested several such mechanisms. They included:

- Reinstating a procedure of presecurity clearance for scientists and engineers with the proper credentials
- Instituting a special visa category for established scientists, engineers, and health researchers
- Involving the U.S. scientific and technical community in determining areas of particular security concern

"The U.S. research community can assist consular officials by providing appropriate documentation for those foreign citizens who are engaged in collaborations with our scientists and engineers," the statement said.[26]

Such proposals are worthy of consideration, as are others. It is clear that American businesses and communities are facing an unintended consequence of the war against terrorism. Many businesses, including the member firms of Deloitte, rely on the free flow of people and professional skills to drive their businesses. Unless we see a change in the flow of much-needed intellectual capital, the United States runs the risk of lagging behind rather than leading the world.

THE CHALLENGES OF GLOBALIZATION: A MATTER OF POLICY

The challenges of globalizing have created business risks that are expansive and potentially of very high impact.

In my meetings with CEOs, one idea dominates: The war on terror can be effectively waged by the United States only as part of a broad coalition of nations. Not to do so will put the United States and its economic players at greater risk and render us susceptible to competitive disadvantage for decades to come. Jim Orr, the CEO of Convergys, made a simple point that is worth repeating: "The United States is too insular." We must reach out and better understand the world, not demand that the world understand us.

This is not to suggest that we abdicate our position of leadership in the global arena. But anyone who has ever been involved in team sports knows that winning is a matter of motivating all team members, from the third-string backup player to the starters, to work together as well as do their individual best. People experienced in team sports know, too, that the most significant contributions are often made by someone other than the star.

There is little precedent for the aims of the war on terror as it is now being waged, or for its reliance on such policies as legally sanctioned torture and extraordinary rendition. It's my belief that the United States, and certainly global interests, would be better served by an American foreign policy that places human rights above all other considerations. The United Nations' *Universal Declaration of Human Rights*, now nearly 60 years old, has endured because its principles transcend national differences and narrow corporate interests. Forging a broad coalition to fight the war on terror in a measured fashion, rather than "charge the beaches," as we've done in Iraq, would be in our best interests. It would join us and many nations, most importantly those of the European Union, in common cause and create a force with which terrorists everywhere would have to reckon.

Perhaps singer Bono of U2 was right when he said at Davos, Switzerland, in 2005, that western countries wanted "to be remembered for something other than the war against terrorism."[27] As of this writing, unfortunately, America's image seems to have lost much of the luster that was gained between the end of World War II and the end of the 20th century. "Attitudes toward America are marked by ambiguity and ambivalence, but they have become more negative in recent years," noted a study by the Council of Foreign Relations cited in Chapter Five.[28]

The challenge is clear: to revitalize what advertising and marketing leaders have called the American brand. Perhaps we have entered a new age, when the ability of American companies to prosper abroad will depend on their ability to keep a low profile, at least for the foreseeable future.

NOTES

1. Interview conducted on August 16, 2004.
2. Online Newshour, "Students Stay at Home," June 24, 2004 on *http://www.pbs.org/newshour/bb/education/jan-june04/bowser6-24.html.*
3. Rob Paral and Benjamin Johnson, "Maintaining a Competitive Edge: The Role of Foreign-Born and U.S. Immigration Policies in Science and Engineering," *Immigration Policy in Focus*, vol. 3, no. 3, August 2004. *www.ailf.org/ipc/ipf081804.asp.*

4. Ibid.

5. Lee Hockstader, "Post-9/11 Visa Rules Keep Thousands from Coming to U.S., *Washington Post*, November 11, 2003.

6. Linda K. Wertheimer, "Hurdles for Foreign Students Take Toll on College's Scientific Work," *Dallas Morning News*, December 5, 2002.

7. Council of Graduate Schools, "Findings from 2005 CGS International Graduate Admissions Survey 1." *www. cgsnet.org/portals/0/pdf/R_intlapps05_I.pdf.*

8. Stuart Anderson, "America's Future is Stuck Overseas," Op-ed, *New York Times*, November 16, 2005.

9. National Science Board, "Science and Engineering Workforce: Realizing America's Potential," National Science Foundation, August 14, 2003, p. 9, on *www.nsf.gov/nsb/ documents/2003/nsb0369/nsb0369.pdf.*

10. Linda K. Wertheimer, "Visa Policy Hinders Research," *Dallas Morning News*, November 24, 2002.

11. "Imported Brains," Editorial, *New York Times*, December 3, 2005.

12. Gnanaraj Chellaraj, Keith E. Maskus, and Aaditya Mattoo, "The Contribution of Skilled Immigration and International Graduate Students to U.S. Innovation." *http://spot.colorado.edu/~maskus/papers/patentpaper_ March%2016_2005.pdf.*

13. Bay Area Science and Innovation Consortium (BASIC), "Visas for Higher Education and Scientific Exchanges: Balancing Security and Economic Competitiveness," April 2005. *www.bayeconfor.org/pdf/ VisasforHEdSciEx.pdf.*

14. Ibid.

15. House Committee on the Judiciary, Subcommittee on Immigration, Border Security, and Claims, *Sources and Methods of Foreign Nationals Engaged in Economic and Military Espionage*, 109th, 1st Session, September 15, 2005. Written testimony by Dr. William A. Wulf. Provided by Dr. Wulf.

16. Ibid.

17. Allison Chamberlain, "Science and Security in the Post-9/11 Environment," July 2004. *www.aaas.org/spp/post911/visas/*.

18. Ibid.

19. Graduate Management Admission Council, Press Release, "Growth in MBA Applications Slowed in 2002-03," McLean, VA, July 31, 2003.

20. Tim Pappa, "Foreign MBA Students Dwindle at U.S. Business Schools," *Virginian Pilot*, August 19, 2004.

21. Allison Chamberlain, "Science and Security in the Post-9/11 Environment," July 2004. *www.aaas.org/spp/post911/visas/*; and Christine Szustaczek, "U.S. Border Laws Keep Professor Home," University of Toronto, News@UofT. November 22, 2002. *http://www.news.utoronto.ca/bin3/021122b.asp*.

22. Allison Chamberlain, "Science and Security in the Post-9/11 Environment," July 2004. *www.aaas.org/spp/post911/visas/*.

23. Barry Bergman, "Research Under Fire: In the War on Terror, Academic Freedom Could Wind up as Collateral Damage," *UCBerkeleyNews*, January 27, 2005. *www.berkeley.edu/news/berkeleyan/2005/01/27_acfreedom.shtml*.

24. Tim Pappa, "Foreign MBA Students Dwindle at U.S. Business Schools," *Virginian Pilot*, August 19, 2004.

25. "Imported Brains," Editorial, *New York Times*, December 3, 2005.

26. "Current Visa Restrictions Interfere with U.S. Science and Engineering Contributions to Important National Needs," December 13, 2002. *www8.national academies.org/onpinews/newsitem.aspx?RecordID= s12132002.*

27. "Davos Succumbs to Star Power," January 30, 2005, Deutsche Welle. Accessed at: *www.dw-world.de/dw/ article/0,1564,1473433,00.html.*

28. Craig Charney and Nicole Yakatan, "A New Beginning: Strategies for a More Fruitful Dialogue with the Muslim World," *CSR*, no. 7, May 2005, Council on Foreign Relations. *www.cfr.org/content/publications/attachments/ Anti-American_CSR.pdf.*

PART THREE

THE WAY FORWARD

Once security and risk management are an integral part of the strategic thinking of an organization, business challenges of a different order present themselves. In this section, as a conclusion, I address two issues vital to the post-9/11 world, which also give an important cultural and ethical dimension to issues of corporate security. First, what three fundamentals must corporations execute to achieve sustainability and leadership? Second, what kind of ethical thinking and behavior must inform businesses as they face the opportunities, challenges, and threats of a globalizing world?

As you have gathered from the discussion so far, good questions abound, but off-the-shelf solutions and answers are difficult to find. This book will have succeeded to the extent that it helps its readers answer both the right and the tough questions.

8

LESSONS LEARNED: THE IMPORTANCE OF FUNDAMENTALS

In the course of this discussion, the focus has been on those technical elements of security and risk management that are essential to securing and sustaining the future of corporations. In this chapter, in an effort to situate those findings in a broader context of sustained growth, I want to offer some suggestions about the course of action, or steps, that companies—big or small—need to consider if they are to compete successfully in the local, national, and global arenas.

Typically, we think that being competitive always starts with a great and original idea, but reality is more mundane. The success of competitive companies often lies with simple fundamentals that we know, but that we don't always act on. I thought it best to focus on sustainable competitiveness in three fundamental areas:

1. Measuring performance and sustainability
2. Governance
3. Innovation

MEASURING PERFORMANCE AND SUSTAINABILITY

Let's begin with measuring performance and sustainability—a cornerstone of long-term success. As explained earlier, Deloitte views performance in a broad and balanced framework, where financial results are just one indicator of success. Equally important are nonfinancial indicators. Also explained earlier, nonfinancials represent leading indicators of success, whereas financials are largely a window on the past. Leading indicators include, among others:

- Customer satisfaction
- Product and service quality
- Ethical conduct and reputation
- Operations
- Employees' commitment

Going forward, CEOs who cast themselves as corporate sentinels must discipline themselves to look constantly beyond the bottom line, beyond the next quarter, and beyond short-term market expectations to focus squarely on the future in order to invest and grow sustainably. That kind of disposition will help to secure meaningful returns and sustainable growth for stakeholders for years to come.

Although the study "In the Dark: What Boards and Executives Don't Know about the Health of Their Businesses"[1] found that only 34% of the management group were inclined to say they monitored nonfinancials as well as financials, we should not conclude that all companies are failing to measure sustainable performance. Examples of companies that are attuned to the implications of these indicators in a flat world are to be found everywhere. In India, for example, there are companies already helping to set the global standard in measurement of performance. A good example is Infosys. With a market capitalization of about US$18.5 billion and more than 46,000 employees, Infosys prides itself on its ability to take the measure of its performance and the marketplace. On a weekly basis, it measures about 120 variables, including these:

- Markets
- Technologies
- Customers
- Staff
- Quality
- Productivity at every phase

Because it emphasizes performance, Infosys rewards up to 50% of its employees on the basis of measured performance.[2] This conscious focus on the long term speaks directly to better management through enhanced performance measurement, systematic attention to stakeholders' expectations, and rigorous promotion of sustainable competitiveness.

In sum, measuring performance and sustainability is somewhat like driving. You need to balance carefully the amount of time you look ahead through the windshield with the time you spend looking in the rearview mirror. A failure to do both appropriately will almost invariably lead to an accident.

GOVERNANCE

Now to the second issue—good governance—a subject
that is often in the headlines but is still underappreciated
in terms of the strategic value it can add. Managing risk
and measuring performance are best achieved in a corporate culture and framework that recognize the value of
good corporate governance. Experience tells us that governance models vary and that no single country can claim
to have the best practices. Each system has its strengths
and weaknesses. For some regions, such as Asia, the challenges include managing a governance process in which
there are large majority stakeholders, frequently a family
or the state.

A second issue is a shortage of business management
skills to ensure that company boards are composed of
experienced and independent members. Whatever the cir-
cumstance or country, there is no easy answer. Still,
regardless of the business environment, there are fundamentals or guiding principles for good governance. These
should inform the governance process and the role of all
corporate stakeholders, including management, employees, stockholders, and outside service providers, including auditors, as well as enhance the appropriate level of
transparency.

> Transparency allows stakeholders a clear view of
> processes and structures. A transparent organization
> clearly communicates its activities and goals and
> also encourages feedback and participation. Taken
> together, oversight and transparency can help an

organization avoid crises—and shine a light on a problem before it becomes a crisis. As the investment strategist Warren Buffct has said, it's only when the tide goes out, that you can see who has no clothes on.

—Piet Hoogendoorn, Chairman,
Deloitte Touche Tohmatsu

I would put these principles under two headings: (1) corporate culture and (2) fundamental values. Corporate culture addresses such issues as tone at the top—the behavior of and the good example set by management, especially the CEO's team. It also encompasses matters such as a balanced focus on the interests of all stakeholders, a focus that also ensures appropriate attention to both short-term goals and long-term objectives (a point that was addressed earlier).

Fundamental values must be at the core of a company's governance practices because they are also essential to risk management, as outlined previously. Independence is the foundation of all business judgment and advice. Unless the advisor, board member, or analyst is free of financial interests in a given company, it is very difficult for him or her to provide insight that is not tainted—or at least not perceived as tainted by other stakeholders or third parties. Objectivity is the intention and ability to think critically and challenge accepted wisdom, practice, or convention. Without objectivity, a board or management team loses touch with the interests of its many stakeholders.

Finally, we come to integrity and quality. These two values are the cornerstone of all business sustainability and competitiveness. Without integrity and quality, one loses the trust and confidence of stakeholders and customers alike. And once trust is lost, it is extremely difficult to rebuild.

SHARED VALUES

For its part, as a global organization, Deloitte has four shared values. These shared values bind the people of Deloitte member firms together and promote trust among partners and professionals, allowing them and their member firms to enhance the confidence of the capital markets. These values join together all employees across different cultures, customs, and languages and are the foundation for collective successes.

Carefully identified through a global consultation process, these values are all-encompassing and embrace the cultures in which Deloitte Touche Tohmatsu and its member firms operate. This thorough process resulted in universal shared values that form a basis for a consistent approach to service delivery worldwide. The shared values are:

- Integrity
- Outstanding value to markets and clients
- Commitment to each other
- Strength from cultural diversity

Together with the commitment of the member firms to delivering measurable value for clients, shareholders, and capital markets, these values help set the tone and foundation for sustainable growth for all stakeholders.

INNOVATION

Much of what I have said focuses on issues related to management processes, the foundation of sustainable competitiveness. The third dimension I would like to briefly discuss is innovation. Innovation is critical to sustaining a competitive edge. In the past 50 or so years, most innovation has come from the United States, Europe, or Japan. This almost seems inevitable, given the comparative advantage these countries have enjoyed in terms of education, research labs, funding, regulatory conditions, and an intimate understanding of consumer culture. Today, things are changing, and the tide of innovation is beginning to shift in favor of certain developing economies. India, for example, produces more than 350,000 engineers a year, as well as 3.1 million English-speaking graduates,[3] and India's culture of research and development is emerging, thanks to both domestic and foreign investment.

Now it is not unusual for large Western companies to combine their talents with those found in fast-growing economies. The combined talent of GE's engineers in Germany, China, India, and the United States is responsible for a new generation of wind turbine.[4] Intel developed its new Centrino processor in an Israeli research and development lab.[5]

India and China are attractive sites for research and development because they offer the rare combination of low cost and highly skilled labor. That's why Motorola India was called on to develop inexpensive cell phones for emerging markets, and why most pharmaceutical companies are conducting research—and more early-stage research—in India, where they can realize cost savings of 30% to 50%.[6]

The challenge for the rapidly emerging countries of Asia is how to move from being "fast followers" to being innovators. One critical ingredient in this process is for management to promote "constructive turmoil." Constructive turmoil recognizes that good ideas are not necessarily developed in a linear fashion; nor are they necessarily the monopoly of top leadership. Therefore, it is imperative for management to continue to invest in research, even when the return seems low, and to continue to empower younger managers to think for themselves and nurture a culture of collaboration that challenges traditional thinking.

****

Additionally, let us bear in mind that sustainable competitiveness requires the right balance between creativity and appropriate management processes. Going forward, all companies need to benchmark their performance against the highest global standard and measure their business processes against best practices. At the same time, intangibles such as a strong tone at the top, relevant shared values, and a robust culture rooted in diversity are essential to success. That these factors remain difficult to measure and quantify is all the more reason to pay them extra attention and not dismiss them as soft stuff or the like. In fact, the more a company masters the fundamentals—measuring performance and sustainability, governance, and innovation—the more management and all stakeholders will begin to understand and appreciate success and growth in the broader context of sustainability.

NOTES

1. "In the Dark: What Boards and Executives Don't Know about the Health of Their Businesses," Survey by Deloitte & Touche U.S.A. LLP, in cooperation with the Economist Intelligence Unit, 2004.

2. Infosys Technologies Limited, 2006 Analyst Meeting, November 11, 2005. Cf., "Entering the Fortune 500: How Do Indian Companies Go Global?" Speech by Charlotte Crosswell, Head of NASDAQ International, Delhi, India, November 15, 2005.

3. "Framing the Engineering Outsourcing Debate: Placing the United States on a Level Playing Field with China and India," Duke University, Master of Engineering Management Program, 2005. *http://memp.pratt.duke.edu/downloads/duke_outsourcing_2005.pdf.*

4. "GE Bringing Latest Technology, Global Experience into Asia's Growing Wind Energy Industry," Press Release, November 1, 2004. *www.gepower.com/about/press/en/2004_press/110104a.htm.*

5. "Centrino: Intel's Israeli Savior," *What's Cooking*, July 2006, vol. 6, no. 7. *http://www.computerpoweruser.com/editorial/article.asp?article=articles/archive/c0607/61c07/61c07.asp&guid=.*

6. "The Next Big Thing," *The Economist*, June 16, 2005.

9

SUSTAINABLE LEADERSHIP: IMPERATIVES FOR A NEW CENTURY

In the years since 9/11, American companies have acknowledged a heightened need to safeguard their human, intellectual, and physical assets. Toward that end, more companies are routinely incorporating security planning into strategic decision making and centralizing global security operations under the watchful care of a chief security officer—a position that, for the most part, didn't exist a generation ago. Meanwhile, there are legitimate concerns that the policies and practices designed to keep America safe are also costing it dearly. Since the early days of the republic, America has benefited inestimably from the contributions of foreign nationals who have come here to study, create, and lead. Now, for the first time in its history, America is coming to be viewed less as a beacon of opportunity and hope than as a bureaucratic minefield.

These developments are taking place against a troubling international backdrop. Today, billions of people in developing countries have a choice of ideologies and roads to take. These people want good health, a safe environment, a living wage, and humane working conditions. Most of all, they want a hopeful and secure future for their children. Yet large segments of the world's population have none of these things and no hope of ever attaining them. That degree of deprivation can't help breeding anger and resentment. That reaction, in turn, is exacerbated when unprincipled economic conduct enriches the wealthy at the expense of the poor.

All of us—government institutions, nongovernmental organizations (NGOs), and multinational corporations—are part of the problem. And all of us must be part of the solution. Many corporate managers equate ethical behavior with corporate largesse and giving back—that is, contributing time and resources to community initiatives and nonprofit organizations. But to my mind, giving back has always connoted a we-and-they relationship, not a partnership, with the world at large. It suggests a quid pro quo rather than a shared vision—the price a company must pay for the right to a healthy bottom line. That mind-set is surely inconsistent with the notion of sustainable leadership.

I am talking about ethical behavior that will promote globalization as an ever-growing force for peace and prosperity. Yet, paradoxically, as globalization gains momentum, the most dramatic social change takes place increasingly at the local level. By partnering with the communities where they do business, corporations have an opportunity to ensure that families and individuals are provided with the basic requirements of life—food, housing, education, and health care. Starbucks, for example, has joined forces with a number of corporations, NGOs, and public-sector organizations in working to improve access to clean water in the developing world.

THE GATES MODEL

Perhaps no corporate philanthropic effort is more strategically conceived to build stronger community infrastructures than the Bill & Melinda Gates Foundation. Guided by a belief that "every life has equal value," the Gates Foundation works to reduce inequities and improve lives around the world. In developing countries, it focuses on improving health, reducing extreme poverty, and increasing access to technology in public libraries; in the United States, it focuses on guaranteeing a high-quality education to every child. In recent years, the Gates Foundation has increased its emphasis on microlending—granting loans as small as US$50 to impoverished individuals and grassroots enterprises.

In July 2006, the chairman of Berkshire Hathaway, Warren Buffett, announced that he is donating US$31 billion, representing 68% of his fortune, to the Gates Foundation, which hopes to use the gift to support research and development programs aimed at curing the world's

20 leading diseases, including AIDS.[1] At the time, many wondered why Buffett would have given the money away rather than use it to establish his own foundation. He said he was "not cut out" to be a philanthropist—at least not like the Gateses—and that he preferred to spend his time running his company. "They'll spend more time and energy on it," he told the *New York Times*. "I'm having so much fun doing what I do, and I think they'll be more able to accept any mistakes they made than I would if I made them."[2]

One thing is certain: Initiatives like the Gates Foundation will, in the long run, be more effective than armaments, surveillance programs, and extraordinary rendition in winning the war for democracy. By helping to build stronger communities, they have tangibly greater potential to weaken the appeal of those who would incite and perpetrate terrorism as a means to political and economic enfranchisement.

Make no mistake: American corporations have brought great value to the world economy. They have exported free enterprise, training, capital, and much more. American multinationals also have many incentives to act ethically—from building a brand to building the bottom line. It is no coincidence that the most financially successful companies are those that place the highest premium on social and environmental responsibility. A study by two Harvard Business School professors found that ethics-based companies increased their net income by 756%, versus just 1% for companies that put profit first.[3]

BEYOND PROFIT AND LOSS

It would be erroneous, however, for corporations to view ethical behavior solely through the lens of financial return. Farsighted business leaders recognize that they cannot afford to define their bottom line exclusively in terms of profit and loss, or as separate and distinct from their societal and environmental obligations. These days, it is understood that managing an organization for growth and profitability—any organization, from the largest multinational to the smallest local enterprise—requires the acceptance of a wide scope of social responsibilities. A company's market position and financial growth are largely a reflection of how it addresses such issues as hunger, disease, child labor, and environmental pollution. It cannot cynically mine these concerns for their economic or public relations value. And to abdicate responsibility in these areas on the pretext that profits will suffer is more than merely cynical. It is dangerous.

Admittedly, the actions of corporations these days are constrained by an ever-tighter net of government regulations. But one of the things that came through most clearly and consistently in my meetings with CEOs is that most of them want to go beyond mere compliance. I believe that they support environmental integrity and social responsibility not because this impresses customers and investors, but because it is fundamental to their beliefs and values.

Corporate governance, to be sure, will of necessity play a continuing and dominant role in this regard. Boards of directors are already taking a far more proactive role than ever before in helping companies succeed. They are scrutinizing financial reports, strengthening governance systems, and intensifying their overview of strategy and ethics—all in an effort to build public trust.

Companies must consider corporate governance procedures in light of what I call the spirit of review and renew, because placing governance in the right context means that they view regulation as part of the answer, not the whole answer. Let's not fall into the trap of abiding by the letter of the law while betraying its broader spirit and purpose.

GAUGING SUSTAINABILITY

At Deloitte, financial results are just one indicator of a company's sustainability; strong governance and ethical behavior also contribute significantly to corporate well-being. In fact, financial statements are historical snapshots of a company's past and do not necessarily value or measure sustainability. So much so that Deloitte Touche Tohmatsu is currently developing a tool to help assess sustainability—holistically—across such dimensions as a company's core values, leadership, talent management practices, and impact on the community, to name just a few. For that reason, bolstering the rule of law becomes a powerful motivation for implementing voluntary codes of corporate conduct.

As the foundation of civilized society, the rule of law fosters democracy and makes it possible to have highly efficient markets. Yet today, the rule of law is under attack. From Bali to Baghdad, from Manhattan to Mumbai, we have seen dramatic instances of the rule of law under siege by terrorism. Terrorism, as we have seen in these chapters, is a visible threat to sustainability and to the rule of law. But there are other, less obvious but equally significant, assailants. One of the least visible yet most dangerous is unprincipled economic conduct.

Wherever it occurs, unprincipled conduct exacts a price. Sadly, those who pay the most are those who can afford the least. It's been estimated that if India were "almost free of corruption" by 2010, the average Indian family would earn 22% more.[4] Such an increase would enable 125 million people in India to escape poverty. Greed, corruption, and deceit have also affected the worldwide reputation of America—and its corporations.

NEVER AGAIN THE SAME

Where is the world today? Modern technology has changed our world forever, making it smaller and more connected. Yet the gap between rich and poor has continued to widen. Consider the U.S. federal minimum wage of US$5.15 per hour, which the U.S. House of Representatives has proposed be increased to US$7.25. This would be a windfall for those people who work in developing countries for less than 30 cents per hour.

Such disparities cannot be ignored, nor can the conduct of companies that profit from unprincipled and illegal behavior. To bolster the rule of law, multinational corporations must engage in ethical behavior that promotes greater economic opportunity. Otherwise, the divide between those who have and those who do not will continue to grow—and provide fertile ground for the seeds of hatred and unrest to take root, leading to terrorism.

The reality is that heightened security measures are a critical first step, but the most effective long-term investment we can make in the security of nations is principled economic behavior. The world cannot afford economic misconduct that separates rich and poor, and that serves as a justification for terrorism. For this reason, I strongly believe it is incumbent upon multinational corporations everywhere to lead the world to globalization's next frontier—through principled codes of conduct that bolster the rule of law. Mere compliance with the letter of the law or some baseline code isn't the point. I'm talking about carefully considered codes of conduct that (1) set objective, quantifiable standards; (2) answer first to the moral underpinnings that support all law; (3) use independent monitoring; and (4) require transparent communication with the public.

UNFINISHED BUSINESS

This also goes for the accounting profession, where I have made my living for more than 35 years. I know that many people might raise their eyebrows at the notion of an accounting firm leading the charge for ethical change, but it is a critical priority, both for the Deloitte organization and for its member firms' clients. Deloitte member firms are rules-driven—certainly in the United States—and have always striven to follow the rules. But in the wake of scandals and the loss of investors' confidence, Deloitte must continue to do more to keep building public trust.

In a global environment, principles are important. This is because rules cannot cover all situations, but principles can, by encouraging and demanding responsible action. For some, ethical principles are built into their foundations. For others, that is not the case. But we can all do more.

I would not challenge others to become more ethical without asking the same of my own organization. As you might imagine, this is a vast effort for a network of member firms with 135,000 people in nearly 140 countries. At Deloitte, member firms seek to transform ethical behavior from an implicit norm to an explicit standard:

- Deloitte member firms have established a Global Ethics and Compliance program, and named their first global ethics officer.
- Deloitte has created a global code of conduct, based on nine principles, to unite its people ethically, wherever they may be.
- The code has teeth, specifying for the first time that any member firm or partner who fails to live up to these ethical principles will be subject to expulsion or termination.
- Deloitte member firms will use their global code as an overarching guide in developing their own codes of conduct, giving them the flexibility to address

local regulatory, legal, and cultural requirements, while still meeting the highest standard of global conduct.

While establishing the code is a crucial first step, member firm conduct is far more important. In the words of the first Deloitte Global Chief Ethics Officer, Kjeld Bög, "It's not the paper; it's the behavior that counts." As CEO of Deloitte, I take the responsibility of serving as the example of ethical behavior for Deloitte. I know that I must set the tone if I am to drive my personal commitment to ethical behavior throughout the organization. That is why it is so important to have a set of shared values that articulate the strengths of the organization as well as its aspirations.

Deloitte wants to serve as an example that multinational corporations would be proud to follow. That's important because, going forward, the world has embarked on a struggle between competing voices. The voices that promote democracy and free markets must act ethically if globalization is to succeed. If we don't, the people of developing nations will consider other voices—voices that may promise to feed their children but will do nothing more than feed their anger.

Multinational corporations account today for one-third of the world's gross domestic product (GDP) and two-thirds of world trade; more than half the world's 100 biggest economies are corporations, and the volume of private, transnational capital flows exceeds government development funding in emerging markets by a factor of five, according to the United Nations Development

Program. The impact of the private sector on economic growth, social progress, and the health of the environment has never been greater. Multinationals can be a powerful influence for good, especially in countries whose governments lack a strong tradition of democracy and the rule of law.

Today, it is no longer sufficient for multinational corporations to do merely what is legal, and the business community and its many stakeholders cannot rely on government alone to regulate and protect us from unlawful conduct. Businesses, communities, governments, NGOs, and others must work together in a more systematic and predictable fashion. In every instance, multinational corporations must do what is right—through their conduct, not just their words. It is our duty to act responsibly, and, in doing so, help democracy and free markets become the preferable options for billions of people. We can secure the future of our children only through a global effort and by creating appropriate opportunities for personal growth and training. That kind of action, combined with an integrated security and risk management strategy, will enable companies with the right strategic vision and strong fundamentals to provide sustained leadership and growth for all their stakeholders.

NOTES

1. Carol J. Loomis, "Warren Buffett Gives Away His Fortune," *Fortune*, June 26, 2006.
2. Donald G. McNeil, Jr. "Buffett's Billions Will Aid Fight Against Disease," *New York Times*, June 27, 2006.

3. John P. Kotter and James L. Heskett, *Corporate Culture and Performance* (New York: The Free Press, 1992), p.78.

4. 1998 estimate developed by Ram Ghandi, President of the Indian Merchants Chamber, cited in *International Society of Business, Economics and Ethics*, vol. 1, no. 3, October 2002, p. 2. *http://www.isbee.org/index.php? option=com_docman&task=doc_download&gid=12 &Itemid=39.*

INDEX